CANDYLAND
·IN THE TWIN CITIES·

CANDYLAND

·IN THE TWIN CITIES·

POPCORN, TOFFEE, BRITTLE & BARK

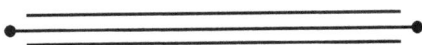

SUSAN M. BARBIERI

AMERICAN PALATE

Published by American Palate
A Division of The History Press
Charleston, SC 29403
www.historypress.net

First published 2014

ISBN 978-1-5402-0968-9

Library of Congress CIP data applied for.

To the tiny girl who loved the ant tunnels, giant bubbles and paper pulp projects at the Children's Museum and going around the corner to get a little bag of jellybeans afterward. May she always live inside you.

Contents

Acknowledgements

Special thanks to David Hanners for tipping me off about this project and to Gary Brueggeman, Roger Wheeler, Rodney Ripley, William Hunt and Robert Kosmalski for sharing their vivid memories of downtown old St. Paul. And a big thank-you to Doug and Brenda Lamb for their patience, their stories and, above all, their dark chocolate haystacks.

Introduction

The aroma is almost tangible enough to require its own calorie-disclosure label. But calories are the last thing on your mind as you follow where your nose leads you on its quest to find the source. You pick up the scent of hot popcorn quick-tossed with a blend of brown sugar, butter and corn syrup. Your olfactory senses detect something else, too—a silky, decadent undercurrent of cocoa. This might be velvety milk chocolate over cashews, bittersweet dark chocolate mixed with finely shredded coconut, caramel and nut snappers bathed in chocolate or rich homemade squares of fudge.

If it's a busy day at Candyland, you stand in line to get in. Then your sense of sight takes over, and it seems you've fallen into a children's picture book where the color palette goes far beyond the basic fairytale rainbow, and every sugary shape seems imbued with whimsy. There's a wall of color-sorted candies. Sugar crystals sparkle from jellied "fruit" wedges and crystal lollipops. Gummy worms practically wriggle in sweet delight behind the clear case. Snowy white sprinkles dust piles of nonpareils.

All of a sudden, you're five years old and don't know where to look first. (Imagine how your child or grandchild feels.) There are speckled jawbreakers the size of billiard balls, cherry- and blueberry-tinted and flavored popcorn balls, Hot Tamales, melt-away mints,

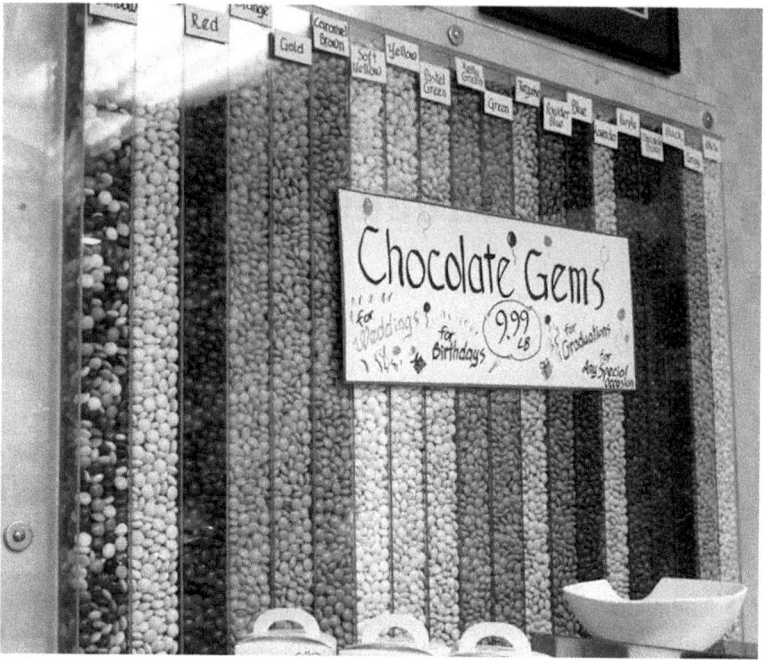

"Chocolate Gems" in rainbow colors.

Tough decision: milk chocolate or dark?

Jellied "fruit" slices dusted in sugar.

pastel taffy chews, roasted nuts, chocolate-dipped pretzels and giant spiral lollipops with ribbons of primary colors.

There's a colorful rhythm to the seasons inside the store. Maybe it's Christmastime, and the gummies and jellies are red and green. Or it's February, and the place is awash in red and pink and you can get chocolate-dipped strawberries for your love. If it's March, treats are shamrock green—if it's April, Easter pastel. July brings patriotic red, white and blue, and October finds the store vivid in crisp, autumnal oranges and reds—accented with a little licorice black for Halloween.

Scientists say that we are hard-wired to crave sugar, fat and salt. The only proof you need is to watch a Candyland "dipper" laboriously coating rippled potato chips in chocolate, one by one, and know that people do buy them.

It seems remarkable that a simple popcorn and candy shop that opened its doors in downtown St. Paul in 1932 during the Great Depression should still be in existence today. Then called Flavo Korn, the store opened at a time when dismal shantytowns dotted the land, and Franklin D. Roosevelt was elected president in the hope that he could solve the country's economic woes. St. Paul was as down-at-the-heels as every other major American city.

For Candyland, survival entailed navigating not only the Great Depression but also a world war, the end of the streetcar system, the decay and eventual demise of the downtown movie palaces and the migration of families to the suburbs. Survival came despite the development of downtown skyway systems that lured pedestrians away from city streets and into climate-controlled walkways. Survival came despite devastating rearrangements of downtown St. Paul's city map, including the development of Interstate 94, which severed the downtown business district from the state capitol and caused potential downtown shoppers to relocate farther away.

When the city closed the old Seventh Street to traffic and created a pedestrian mall between St. Peter and Wabasha Streets just around the corner from Candyland, the Loop that once gave downtown's traffic pattern some cohesion (and young people of the 1950s, '60s and '70s a place to cruise) became fragmented and incoherent. Ask old-timers about the Loop, and they struggle momentarily to reconcile today's downtown with the one that lives in their memories; they will then go on to vividly describe a route that no longer exists that went past landmarks that are long gone.

Any one of these historical developments in downtown St. Paul easily could have killed off a small shop like Candyland; countless other mom and pop stores have come and gone in the past eight

Chocolate-dipped strawberries for Valentine's Day.

decades. There were plenty of reasons for people to abandon downtown. But candy cravings are eternal, and popcorn, it seems, is recession- and depression-proof.

Suburban migration and the advent of television caused dramatic social change after the end of the war, and St. Paul wasn't immune to those trends. In the 1950s, attendance at movie theaters dropped, along with popcorn consumption. But as television became the new "big thing," and people began eating popcorn at home in front of their favorite shows, the snack enjoyed resurgent popularity. The invention and subsequent widespread adoption of the microwave oven gave popcorn yet another boost.

Candyland went from a place frequented by downtown office workers and moviegoers to a destination for those who had moved to the suburbs. Under owners Arnie Kelsey and now Doug and Brenda Lamb, the business survived and thrived, eventually expanding its offerings—although popcorn remains a mainstay of the business to this day.

The colors of autumn and Halloween fun are on display in October.

Chocolate-dipped Peeps are lined up like soldiers and ready to roll around Easter.

Customers no longer buy popcorn to carry into the glittering movie palaces, but old-timers who remember doing so still visit Candyland. Often they're great-grandparents toting little ones. Parents who come to downtown St. Paul with young children to play at the Minnesota Children's Museum or the Science Museum of Minnesota commonly include a stop at Candyland as part of the outing. And although the stenographers, insurance salesmen, theater ushers, streetcar drivers and switchboard operators are long gone, downtown office workers still gravitate to the store looking for a crunchy or sweet snack.

Turn your mind's eye to this storefront on Wabasha Street in downtown St. Paul and imagine a time-lapse film speeding you backward through the decades, from color to grainy black-and-white to sepia, where one little treat store has seen history unfold right outside its door.

CHAPTER 1

Flavo Korn

Popcorn was popular from the 1890s into the years of the Great Depression, when street vendors pushing steam- or gas-powered poppers would follow crowds around at fairs, parks and expositions. During the Depression, popcorn at five or ten cents a bag was one of the few luxuries that financially stressed families could afford. So while other small businesses failed, popcorn businesses thrived. Still, you'd have to be a little crazy or afflicted with a certain blind optimism to want to open a popcorn store in the middle of an economic depression in a city center crawling with famous visiting gangsters and run-of-the-mill local lowlifes. But such was the state of downtown St. Paul when Flavo Korn opened at 453 Wabasha in the Riviera Theater building in 1932.

The country was three years past the Black Tuesday stock market crash of 1929 but still in the iron grip of the worst economic depression in American history. There were fifteen thousand men out of work in St. Paul—affecting one out of every five families. Homeless and jobless men camped out in the city's parks and went door to door through the residential districts seeking meals from compassionate housewives. People seeking relief at the Ramsey County government offices stood four abreast in a line extending for two blocks down Wabasha Street.

The Flavo Korn Shop, photographed in 1938 after Arnie Kelsey and Arvin Flaskerud bought the store from A.L. Mace.

Not much is known about the couple that started Flavo Korn; the names of these two have been lost to the vagaries of time. Only their initials appear on fragile, yellowed business documents from the 1930s: A.L. Mace, who never actually worked the store, and his wife, F.M., who ran the business. In those days, movie theaters didn't have the giant concession areas we have today at the multiplex. Flavo Korn catered to the downtown movie crowd and was perfectly situated to sell bags of the snack to people, who would then carry their popcorn into the theater.

Downtown St. Paul glittered with movie palaces, most of them clustered around Seventh and Wabasha. Before urban renewal, before downtown streets were redrawn, Seventh Street ran along the street today known as Seventh Place, the brick-paved one-block pedestrian mall extending between St. Peter and Wabasha. Seventh and Wabasha buzzed with activity—streetcars, autos, crowds of pedestrians—especially at night. You could stand on the corner facing east and see, half a block down Seventh, the Paramount and Orpheum. Looking north up Wabasha was the Riviera at the end of the block on the left and the Tower and Strand on the right. Farther up the street were the Lyceum and the World.

Whether because of low ticket prices, publicity stunts and wacky promotions or because people simply needed a diversion from the grimness of everyday life during economic hard times, the movie houses actually enjoyed a robust business by the mid-1930s. Indeed, some of the movies still beloved today as classics would have been lighting up the marquees in those years: *Grand Hotel* (1932), *King Kong* (1933), *Top Hat* (1935), *Snow White and the Seven Dwarfs* (1937) and *Gone with the Wind* (1939). Moviegoers would stop in at Flavo Korn for treats to carry into the theater, until theater owners got wise to the profit potential of popcorn and candy.

Box office receipts, which had plummeted during the early years of the Depression, bounced back in 1934 and continued to climb. But a better contributor to theaters' bottom line during the Depression was a new focus on the concession stand. "Candy had always been part of the movie-going experience, but it was almost always sold at a nearby confectionary—not in the theater itself," wrote Dave Kenney in *Twin Cities Picture Show.* He continued:

Theater operators began eyeing the tantalizing profits that could come from the sale of sweets. By 1936 candy sales at the nation's movie theaters—which had accounted for virtually nothing a decade before—exceeded ten million dollars…By the end of the 1930s, Twin Cities theater operators were beginning to cash in on what would soon become an even bigger moviegoing staple: popcorn. Cheaper than other treats, popcorn was one food that Americans actually ate more of during the Great Depression, and movie theaters were largely responsible for feeding the habit. And with more demand came more supply. Between 1934 and 1940, the nation's popcorn harvest grew from 5 million pounds to more than 100 million pounds.

FLAVO KORN IN GANGSTERVILLE

With the increasing competition from the theaters, this would have been a tough time to be running a popcorn shop. Indeed, records show that the Maces made very little money from Flavo Korn in the six years that they owned the place. However, there might have been more changing hands at the little store than quarters for small bags of popcorn. The story passed on to current Candyland owners Doug and Brenda Lamb is that federal agents visited the shop for years asking about A.L. Mace's whereabouts and looking to question him about alleged money laundering.

That sort of activity would have been relatively minor compared to the other illicit activities going on in St. Paul in the early 1930s. Wabasha Street was notorious in those days, a sort of gangster alley extending from the Wabasha caves and the infamous Castle Royale nightclub on the south shore of the Mississippi River, up past the Riviera and Strand theaters to the notorious Green Lantern speakeasy at 545½ Wabasha, about one block north of Flavo Korn and the Riviera.

A who's who of American gangsters hung out in St. Paul in those days. Al Capone kept an apartment in the old World Theater—today the Fitzgerald, home of *A Prairie Home Companion*. Lester Gillis—also known as George "Baby Face" Nelson—and his wife holed up at the St. Francis Hotel on Seventh and Wabasha, the building in which Candyland is located today.

Other visiting criminals included John Dillinger, George "Machine Gun" Kelly, Alvin "Creepy" Karpis and the Ma Barker Gang. Bank robbers, bootleggers, kidnappers and murderers knew that they could lie low in St. Paul, thanks to a police protection racket run by Chief John O'Connor of the St. Paul Police Department. The crooks were welcome in St. Paul as long as they checked in with the police and didn't draw attention to themselves (that part of the bargain inevitably would fall apart). Thugs from Illinois, Texas, Nevada and elsewhere touched base with their contacts at the police department. Bribes were exchanged—Green Lantern proprietor Harry Sawyer was an intermediary between his gangster pals and the police—and the crooks avoided harassment until they lapsed into headline-grabbing crime sprees.

In his autobiography, former Alcatraz Penitentiary resident Alvin Karpis wrote, "Of all the Midwest cities, the one I knew best was St. Paul, and it was a crook's haven. Every criminal of any importance in the 1930s made his home at one time or another in St. Paul. If you were looking for a guy you hadn't seen for a few months, you usually thought of two places—prison or St. Paul."

After prohibition ended in 1933, crooks had to find other things to do to make up for the lost revenue from the bootleg liquor trade. Among the Barker/Karpis Gang's more brazen crimes were the kidnappings of local luminaries William Hamm of Hamm Brewing and banker/brewing company heir Edward Bremer. With the kidnappings grabbing front-page headlines in the newspapers on a daily basis, the city eventually cracked down on the police department. J. Edgar Hoover's Federal Bureau of Investigation (FBI) also was watching the criminal goings-on in St. Paul and had been pursuing Karpis and the Barkers. The kidnapped heirs were eventually freed and the gangsters tried and convicted. By 1936, the big players were in prison, and St. Paul's gangster era was over.

Shortly after Flavo Korn changed hands in 1938, federal agents came around looking for A.L. Mace. Second owner Arnie Kelsey saw Mace only once or twice, including the day he closed escrow on Flavo Korn. "When Arnie bought the store in 1938, it was barely doing any sales," said Doug Lamb. "A month after he bought it, the feds were at his door looking for this guy [Mace]. And that went on for two years, and they kind of assumed Arnie knew something about this guy."

Arnie and Arvin on Theater Row

Arnold Ray Kelsey knew popcorn. His family grew it on their farm near Spencer, Iowa, due south of Albert Lea, Minnesota. Popcorn— or *Zea mays everta*—is a particular variety of corn whose pericarp (hull) has just the right thickness to allow it to burst open into a fluffy snack. Arnie didn't want to take over the family farm. Rather than grow popcorn, he wanted to pop it and sell it.

He got in his car one day and drove up to Albert Lea, which seemed like a happening town compared to rural Spencer, to scout out locations for a shop. Together with his older brother, Paul, he opened a store in Albert Lea but soon determined that there wasn't enough money to be made there. Instead, he cast his eye northward toward St. Paul—downtown St. Paul, where people flocked to movie theaters, office buildings and department stores and where the streetcars would carry customers almost right to his door.

He came up to the city for a visit and found a little popcorn shop for sale on Wabasha Street in the heart of the theater district. He decided to close the Albert Lea location and move to St. Paul to settle down and go into business with his friend Arvin Flaskerud, who worked full time at the St. Paul Fire and Marine insurance company (later the St. Paul Companies). Arnie was twenty-three years old when he and Arvin bought Flavo Korn on September 2, 1938, for $1,000—$300 down and an agreement to pay $50 per month. Interestingly, the pronoun used throughout the real estate document notes the seller as "she," and the signatory was not Mr. Mace, but his wife.

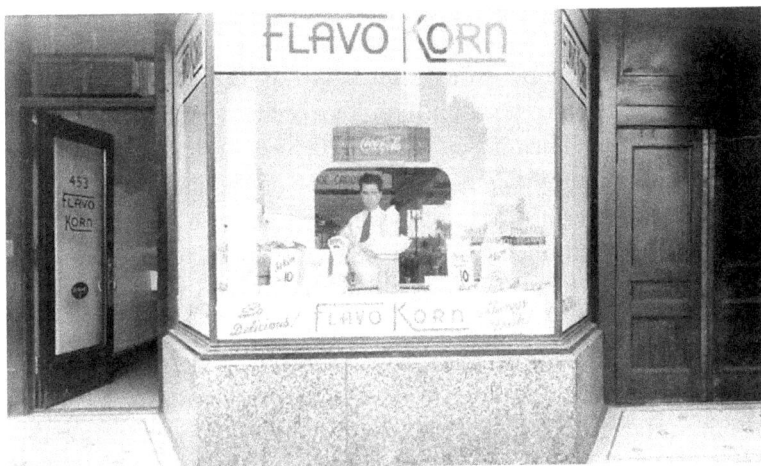

Arnie Kelsey in the window of his Flavo Korn store in 1938. The store originally was housed in the Riviera Theater building.

The purchase included equipment listed on the bill of sale: one popper and basket, a table, a copper kettle, a furnace, a butter popcorn table (steam), an electric nut case, one candy case, one fountain and equipment, one root beer barrel, one cash register, two scales, two iceboxes, three malted milk mixers, one electric clock, one radio, one mirror, one gas stove and light fixtures.

Arnie worked days and Arvin nights. Besides popcorn and fudge made from a recipe of Arnie's, they sold root beer and cola to the movie crowd. Most of the movie houses near Flavo Korn—the Strand, Tower and Riviera on Wabasha and the Orpheum and Paramount on Seventh—had evolved from presenting live theater and vaudeville in the early 1900s to showing Hollywood movies in the 1930s and 1940s. Flavo Korn was located right in the thick of the action near the corner of Eighth (now West Seventh) and Wabasha in the Riviera building—about where the entrance to the Minnesota Children's Museum is today.

For four decades, the Orpheum and its elite competitor across the street, the Paramount, were the top first-run movie theaters in St. Paul. Construction of the Orpheum began in 1915, and it opened as the Palace Theatre in 1916 as a vaudeville house that hosted acts such as Charlie Chaplin and the Marx Brothers. It seated three thousand people, who got unobstructed views of the stage under ornate stuccowork and vaulted ceilings. Across the street, the Paramount Theater, built in 1920, was designed specifically as a motion picture theater. The exterior of the Paramount was a fanciful, Spanish-inspired architectural confection of terra cotta, iron and bronze punctuated with columns, cherubs and gargoyles. Inside, the lobby had a grand dome ceiling and the rich Italian marble befitting a motion picture Versailles.

Across the street from Flavo Korn, the Tower was "a poor man's picture palace," as Dave Kenney described it. With a capacity of about 1,100, its niche was showing quality films at a reasonable price. "The Tower is not gaudy or overdeveloped from an artistic standpoint," according to *Moving Picture World*, an industry trade journal that published from 1907 to 1927. "It impresses one as being lastingly beautiful because of its artistic simplicity." In the 1930s, movie house operators began offering double features to draw more customers, and the Tower continued to show two films for a bargain price even after business picked up during World War II.

A few doors north of the Tower was the Strand, built in the early 1930s and boasting a sleek, bold Art Deco marquee that curved around the corner of Wabasha and Eighth and was topped with a towering, vertical neon sign. Flavo Korn's immediate neighbor, the Riviera, was among the lower-tier, "move-over" movie houses—a theater that got the big Hollywood films once those films had completed their initial runs at the better venues, which in Flavo Korn's neighborhood meant the Palace/Orpheum and the Paramount.

Retiree Roger Wheeler of Shoreview, Minnesota, worked as an usher at the Riviera Theater as a high school student in 1942 and remembered walking past Flavo Korn every day on his way to work. Whenever he catches a whiff of caramel corn at a mall, it reminds him of those days when he'd pass by Arnie's shop. "Quite a few people would go in there and buy things and go in to the movie next door," he recalled. "At the Riv, we had a candy case in the mezzanine or lobby but never had any popcorn or anything extensive like that." At a certain point, the Riviera's owners decided

Flavo Korn shop, 1938. *From left*: Arnie Kelsey and Arvin Flaskerud with one of their first employees.

that it wasn't worth trying to compete with Arnie's products and allowed patrons to bring in his popcorn.

"There were several of us from Johnson High School who had jobs at the various theaters," Wheeler recalled. "Earl was at the Strand, I was at the Riv, Danny was at the Tower. We were all at the various theaters. We had to wear uniforms back then— dickies with paper collars and bow ties. We could get into any theater with our girlfriend if we wanted to because we knew all the guys who were in charge."

The Strand and the Tower had B-movies such as cowboy and monster flicks. The Paramount, Orpheum and Riviera had the class-A movies, Wheeler recalled. Fancier theaters like the Orpheum and the Paramount also had doormen out front attired in long dress coats during the wintertime, and their job was to direct movie patrons into the line for tickets and bark out the start time for the show. If you were a young man who wanted to impress a date, you took her to the Orpheum or the Paramount.

At the end of the night, the ushers had to lug heavy film cans loaded with movie reels over to the Paramount for storage. "That's where we had to drop them off, and they were so heavy. I don't know what they weighed, but boy your arms would just get so tired carrying them over there," Wheeler recalls. "After work, Walgreens had a big drugstore on the corner of Seventh and Wabasha, so we'd either be in there or the St. Francis Hotel across the street to keep warm until the streetcar came. You had what they called the 'twelve o'clock lineup.' All the streetcars from various neighborhoods would line up at twelve o'clock, 12:30 a.m. and so on. It was a very lively place, downtown on Saturday nights."

Twin Cities moviegoers who wanted to see the latest films as soon as they came out had little choice but to go downtown, Kenney wrote. "The best first-run films opened at the best downtown theaters, and they stayed at those theaters as long as they continued to draw big crowds. When a film finished its initial downtown run, it moved to another venue."

The prestigious downtown houses, with their first-run motion pictures and sumptuous surroundings, were considered the glamour spots of the local movie trade. And because they were expensive to own and operate, well-financed companies or individuals typically ran them. By the end of World War II, nearly all of the first-run movie theaters in the Twin Cities were owned by one of two national motion picture firms: in the St. Paul theater district, Paramount Pictures, through its Minnesota Amusement Company (Maco) subsidiary, owned the Paramount, Strand and Tower, while RKO owned the Orpheum. Maco would later pick up ownership of the Riviera as well.

COMPETITION FROM THE BIG BOYS

Arnie and Arvin had plenty of competition from these entertainment behemoths, which had begun adding concession stands in earnest during the Depression. So they focused on selling

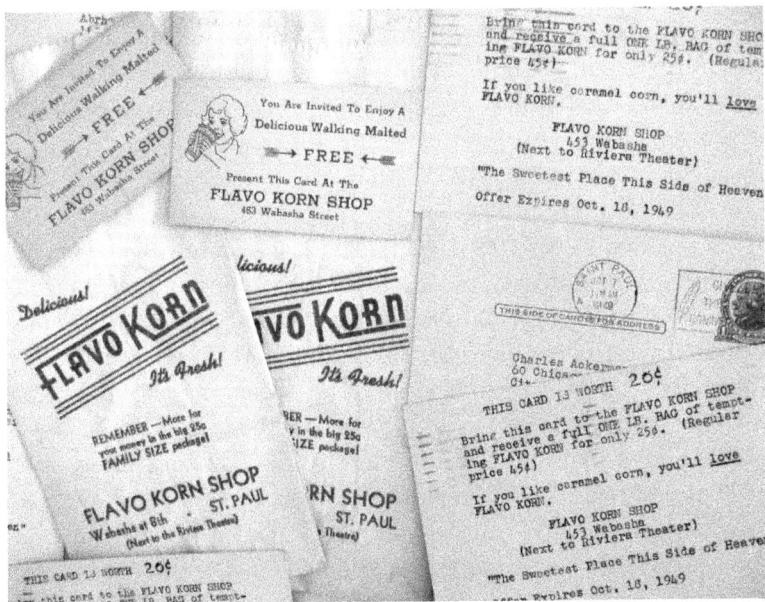

Arnie Kelsey's promotional items from the 1940s included postcards mailed to customers offering twenty cents off a forty-five-cent bag of popcorn at "The Sweetest Place This Side of Heaven." *Photo by author.*

a superior product, and discerning moviegoers soon figured out that Flavo Korn's popcorn was far superior to that being sold at the theater concession stands.

Flavo Korn offered three kinds of popcorn: buttered, cheese corn and caramel corn. Arnie and Arvin stocked other items according to demand or whim—sometimes they sold hard candy and sometimes cigarettes. Other times there were salted nuts and root beer floats. Snack and beverage items came and went, but popcorn at fifteen to twenty-five cents a bag remained the constant. In those pre-supersize days, popcorn was sold in bags that were only slightly larger than a business-size envelope.

Arnie and Arvin were good friends as well as business partners. They even went in together on a brand-new car in May 1941—a Dodge coupe for $50.00, paid in installments of $6.25. But a few years into the partnership, the men decided that there wasn't enough money in the Flavo Korn business to support two families. Since Arvin had a solid full-time job, he offered to bow out and sold Arnie his share of the business for $1.00. Still, with a family to support, it was difficult for Arnie to make a living, and uncertainty was in the air as war drew near. Worse, the theater concession stands were encroaching on his business.

On November 27, 1941, Arnie or his wife rolled a sheet of onionskin paper into a typewriter and wrote to the landlord at mega-theater owner Minnesota Amusement Company, which had recently acquired the Riviera Theater and the building's retail tenants. He asked the recipient, a Mr. Wilson, to do something about the rent increase on his business from $175 per month to $200.

"I feel that that much rent is entirely out of line for the type of my business, especially in that my trade depends to a great extend [*sic*] on your theaters in the vicinity, and you know yourself that the theater business isn't what it should be. They are also cutting into the business a lot by adding candy and even a popcorn machine in their lobbies," he wrote. "I have felt all the time that $175.00 was pretty steep, but $200.00 is entirely too much for this size of a place with its location. I have contacted both A.L. Shinners Agency and the Nienaber Agency regarding selling my business, but neither of them care much about handling it with that much rent because they don't think it would be possible to sell this type of a business for a place with so much rent."

Before long, world events would make a twenty-five-dollar-per-month rent increase seem trivial indeed.

CHAPTER 2

Seventh and Wabasha
in the 1940s

As America entered World War II, Arnie and his buddy Arvin left for boot camp and then Europe. Arnie was shipped off with the army to France, where he wound up working in the PX selling Hershey bars. While the men were away, Beryl Kelsey ran the store with help from Muriel Flaskerud, making do amid sugar shortages, shorter movie queues and a generally depressed business climate downtown. While many women during the war stepped up and did jobs that had been considered primarily men's work, at mom and pop businesses, the only break from routine was that the women took over all aspects of running the stores.

With her husband away, Beryl Kelsey was the one who now dealt with popcorn suppliers and confectioners, the U.S. government rationing office and the occasional visits from federal agents who continued to stop in periodically to ask about the whereabouts of A.L. Mace. Doug remembered Beryl Kelsey as a woman more than capable of managing the store. "Beryl ran the business during wartime," he says. "She was hardcore. She was tough. Arnie was not so tough."

As soon as the United States entered the war in the winter of 1941–42, air raid shelters were set up in the Twin Cities, and victory gardens last seen during World War I again sprouted in the city.

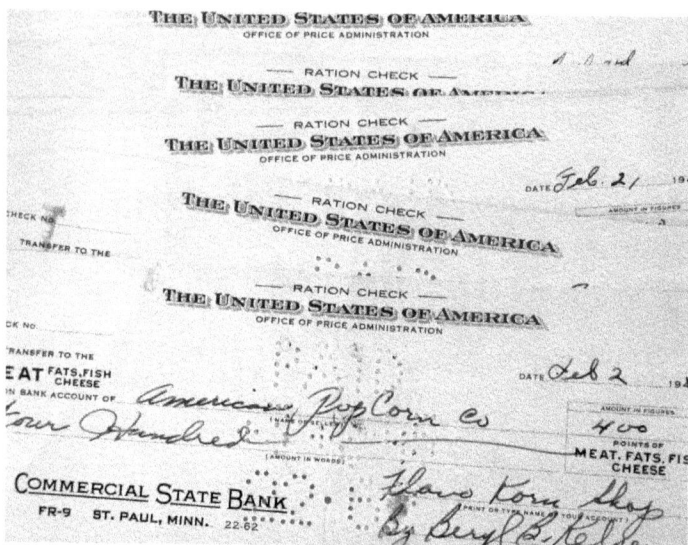

Canceled wartime ration checks written out to popcorn and candy suppliers. *Photo by author.*

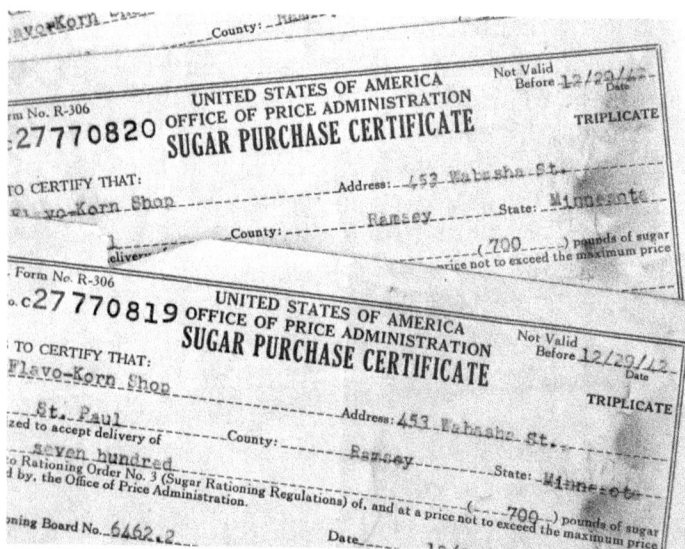

During World War II, Flavo Korn needed special certificates from the government to purchase bulk quantities of rationed sugar. *Photo by author.*

Additional streetcars were put into service to meet the demand that gas rationing created once people were no longer able to fill up their cars. The popular No. 1 streetcar line that ran east–west and spilled riders out onto Seventh and Wabasha enjoyed a bump in ridership as people took to mass transit again.

A food rationing and price control system was established to provide resources needed for the war and to avoid the kinds of economic problems that had resulted during World War I, such as high inflation. This time around, government programs for rationing and price controls were administered at the local level by the Office of Price Administration (OPA), and virtually every household was affected.

By 1943, every citizen was asked to do his or her patriotic duty and cut back on meat, sugar, coffee, canned foods, fuel, shoes and consumer goods. Sugar was the first food to be rationed in the spring of 1942. The war with Japan cut off U.S. imports from the Philippines, and cargo ships from Hawaii were diverted for military purposes. The nation's supply of sugar was quickly reduced by more than one-third. To prevent hoarding and skyrocketing prices, the Office of Price Administration issued 123 million copies of War Ration Book One, which contained stamps that could be used to purchase sugar. No sugar could legally be bought without stamps, and sugar rationing would continue until supplies returned to normal in 1947.

Popcorn businesses managed to keep their doors open during World War II, while businesses that focused on selling confections went out of business because of the sugar rationing. Unable to snack on sweets, people turned to salty snacks such as popcorn for their treat fix—in fact, Americans ate three times as much popcorn as usual during the war.

Among the mementos that Arnie Kelsey kept in an army-green eleven- by seven-inch metal box were canceled ration checks signed by Beryl and Muriel for raw goods and popcorn and receipts from suppliers such as the American Popcorn Co., Tilden Brothers, Barnard Popcorn Supply, R.L. Gould & Co. and Pan Confection Factory. The Pan Confection receipt lists purchases of licorice creams, "juju wee bits," mint lozenges and chocolate nut assortments by the carton. Yellowed Flavo Korn advertisements from the 1940s

Arnie Kelsey saved some World War II items in an army-green metal box that he gave to the Lambs. In it were canceled ration checks, ration account deposit slips and other wartime documents. *Photo by author.*

weren't big on artistry or punctuation but featured a product photo and an attempt at humor: "Picture of my WALNUT FUDGE which I sell to people for 29c lb. You don't have to hunt for the nuts." And, "Picture of my ENGLISH TOFFEE which I sell to people for 49c lb. You can't afford it but it's awful good. Very tasty."

While women kept things running on the homefront, St. Paul servicemen not only dreamed of their gals back home but also nurtured fond memories of the most exciting corner in downtown St. Paul. In columns written in the 1950s, *St. Paul Pioneer Press* journalist Gareth Hiebert, whose "Oliver Towne" columns often took the tone of romantic odes to the city, described the special place Seventh and Wabasha held in the hearts of St. Paul servicemen:

> *We are told that when the boys in service during World War II*
> *and again in the Korean conflict requested pictures of St. Paul,*

the place they wanted to see most was Seventh and Wabasha. Other corners and intersections in the city may have a claim to fame, but Seventh and Wabasha has long been a favorite. In each 24 hours, it plays a variety of roles and is the stage for untold real life dramas. "Meet me at Seventh and Wabasha" is like saying in New York City, "I'll See You Under the Biltmore Clock."

Fresh Start: Flavo Korn Reborn

Arnie and Arvin both returned home in mid-1942 and resumed their working lives in downtown St. Paul, but times would remain tough for a few more years. It was a while before they started getting supplies again, Doug Lamb said. The store made only $2,900 per year during wartime, according to tax returns.

"Sales were terrible," he noted. "People weren't around. All the nightlife went away. People couldn't get product; people couldn't get supplies. Downtown was the place to go, and all of a sudden there's nothing downtown. People weren't coming downtown. A lot of people were hurt by it. There were a lot of businesses—he was next to Alary's Bar on one side and Lighthouse Bakery on the other—and the bakery didn't make it. They closed up. And from that point on, it was a number of businesses that came and went."

Nevertheless, the holidays must have been busy enough at Flavo Korn because in November and December 1944, Arnie hired several women to work at the store. The women had old-fashioned names, the kind that haven't yet cycled back into fashion: Gertrude, Evelyn, Bernice and Jean. Their W4 forms and other wartime employee forms are among the oddball World War II items that Arnie saved in his metal box. Also stashed in the box were wartime ration tickets, recipes and equipment lists. There are also promotional postcards addressed to customers by name, street address and simply "City." There was no need to be specific; in the 1940s, the downtown St. Paul Post Office knew which "City."

INSTRUCTIONS FOR 1943 DECLARATION FORM 1040-ES
AND
TABLE FOR ESTIMATING TAX ON INCOMES OF NOT OVER $10,000

These instructions and table are furnished for the convenience of taxp...
their Income and Victory Tax for the purpose of the Declaration. Taxp...
pute their tax more precisely can obtain from the Collector of Int...
work sheet with more detailed instructions.

Calendar Year
1943

WHO MUST ...

...ation must be made by every citize...
...d States if he comes within

STATEMENT OF VICTORY TAX WITHHELD
By Employer
(EMPLOYEE'S RECEIPT)

...GLE OR MARRIE...
...rescribed fo...

...MENT
...CE

...PLOYER
duplicate for
...hom Victory
...eld. Furnish
(See Instruc-
...t Victory Tax
V-1.) Forward
...rn of Victory Tax
...1, for the fourth
...r (or with the em-
...r if filed at an

EMPLOYEE
TO WHOM
PAID

(Print full name of employee, home address, and social security number, if any. If employee is a married woman, name of husband should also be furnished)

EMPLOYER
BY WHOM
PAID

(Name and address of employer)

STATEMENT OF VICTORY TAX WITHHELD
remuneration paid during the calendar year 1943, or, if for
...ar year, from _____ to _____

$ _____

$ _____

During World War II, employers withheld a "victory tax" from employee paychecks. Arnie Kelsey saved many of these wartime documents. *Photo by author.*

When the war finally ended, St. Paul residents converged on Seventh and Wabasha, the city's unofficial town square, to celebrate. *St. Paul Pioneer Press* reporter Elliott Tarbell captured the mood when thousands of people spontaneously descended on this part of downtown as the war came to an end on August 14, 1945:

> *A group of servicemen clambered atop a parked automobile at Seventh and Wabasha and opened a quart bottle of whisky with lusty whoops. The laughing crowd cheered, automobile horns began honking, accompanied by the shouts of the crowd. The Seventh and Wabasha corner was the center of the loop demonstration. A jalopy occupied by some teen-age youths started circling around the block. Other cars followed. In no time the cars joining this impromptu parade were too many for a single line, and drivers started circling the block two abreast to the constantly increasing din from their horns and shouts from*

*gay celebrants loosening up to the spirit of the occasion more as
each minute passed...*

*Within an hour or so the din was general over the loop with
merrymakers parading their cars through the streets with an
abandon that ignored completely all the lean years of rationed
gasoline and tires...And as the celebrants circled giddily around
block after block they were showered with confetti, torn-up bits of
newspapers, ticker tape and anything else that persons leaning out
of office windows found convenient to toss at them.*

Arnie's Flavo Korn store was in the thick of the downtown
action as that spontaneous motorcade sparked what would
become a regular postwar weekend leisure activity for young
people: cruising the Loop. And as sugar and other supplies
gradually started to become plentiful again, business picked up at
the downtown movie theaters. Among the films that would have
been showing in St. Paul's theater district were Hollywood hits
such as *Meet Me in St. Louis* (1944), *The Bells of St. Mary's* (1945)
and *Easter Parade* (1948).

Retired civil engineer Rodney Ripley of Spooner, Wisconsin,
lived in St. Paul in the 1940s and early 1950s and remembered that
downtown St. Paul was the place to be in those years. "The streetcars
used to go up that West Seventh and Wabasha intersection there,
and it was said that if you stood at the corner of Wabasha and West
Seventh, eventually you would meet everybody in St. Paul. That was
the center of activity because at night, that's where the streetcars
lined up after midnight to serve the movie crowd," said Ripley, who
remembered watching cowboy movies at the second- and third-
tier downtown theaters and then catching a clattery, clangy yellow
streetcar for the ride home.

Arnie fervently wished that his store had been located on that
corner, closer to the prestigious first-run theaters that drew the
big crowds. But there were no available retail spots in that prime
location, so he rebranded his business in the hopes that more of
those potential customers would walk down the block to his door.

In the late 1940s, Arnie changed the name of the store to
Candyland and added the sweet treats that had been so missed

during the war. But like many who lived through the Depression, he would never be able psychologically to leave the lean years completely behind, even into the 1970s.

"He never had napkins on the counter," owner Brenda Lamb recalled. "Arnie worked part time for us for two years before he fully retired. And I said, 'Why don't you have napkins available?' We would put them in the bags. And he said, 'Well, since the Depression they rationed all the paper products because everything had to go overseas. I never put them out again, ever.'"

CHAPTER 3

Candyland on the Loop

Arnie's business was good at Candyland in the years after the war. Popcorn and nuts continued to sell well, but the old Riviera building had no air conditioning system, so the availability of chocolates depended largely on the weather. It was too risky to stock chocolates in the summertime, so he only carried hard candies until the fall, when the temperature cooled off.

"The '50s and '60s are when things really started taking off for the store," Brenda Lamb said. "Products were back in stock, and he did very well. Downtown was the place to be. You didn't have the suburbs yet taking off. Everybody came downtown for entertainment, their doctor's appointments, shopping—everything was involved around the downtown area. Movies—we had eleven movie theaters at one point in the downtown area, and they weren't small. They were pretty nice size, one screen, beautifully built theaters. So that was the place to go. They'd buy popcorn at the theater, but they would also buy it and bring it in."

Like many young people who hung out in downtown St. Paul in the late '40s and early '50s, retiree Robert Kosmalski of St. Paul remembered Candyland, but often he didn't have the spare nickels and dimes to spend there. In fact, buddies who worked as ushers often snuck Kosmalski and his friends into the movies for free. He remembers going to 3D movies at the Riviera—in 1953, the first major 3D film, *Bwana Devil*, set attendance records at the theater. Soon came *House of Wax*, *Kiss Me Kate* and *It Came from Outer Space*—all in 3D. But the fad petered out within a year.

"The best movies were at the Paramount and the Orpheum, and the musicals, which all of the girls would go to, and that's where us guys would go in the hopes of picking up some dollies. But we never were successful. And then after the movies, of course, Candyland was there with their caramel corn," said Kosmalski.

He remembered Victor Costello, whose newsstand was a fixture at the corner of Seventh and Wabasha outside the lobby of the St. Francis Hotel. "Saturday nights, the people would drive by in their cars, and he'd be selling the early edition of the Sunday paper right through the car window, and it was just fantastic to watch him," he recalled.

Seventh and Wabasha was "the center of the universe," and the streetcar stop going east was so jam-packed that it was difficult to get in and out of Walgreens, Kosmalski noted. "It was a great life to go bummin' downtown. When we got to the age to be able to drive cars, not very many had cars, and we would pool our money for gas money, and five or six or seven of us would jump in a car and drive downtown and pick up girls. And we never were successful there, either."

Arnie continued to keep his eye out for an opportunity to move Candyland a few doors down, although the postwar years were about to bring major changes to his corner of downtown that threatened to make it difficult to stay in business, let alone move or expand.

Moviegoing had peaked nationwide in 1946 and was starting to decline. Young people who had once spent their time and money at the movies were now busy getting married, buying homes, having babies and spending their money on appliances and other items that had been unavailable during the war. And the homes they were outfitting tended to be in the suburbs, where multiplexes and television held a lot more appeal than the beautiful old movie houses downtown. Box office receipts were down, as was the amount of money that the average American spent going out to the movies. Amid dwindling attendance, a dozen theaters in Minneapolis and St. Paul shut down in 1951 and 1952.

There were potential customers coming downtown in those days, but if their skin was the wrong color, they couldn't spend their money at some of the stores. In her book *Days of Rondo*, Evelyn Fairbanks described what it was like to be a black teenager in St. Paul in the 1950s trying to enjoy the same downtown shopping and dining experience as white teens:

> *Some of the places, such as Walgreen's drugstore on Seventh and Wabasha, did not openly deny service; they just waited on us last at the lunch counter. We may have only wanted Cokes, but by the time they took our orders, we asked for a full meal. When we saw the waitress bringing the food, we would get up and walk out, leaving the restaurant with a full meal to throw away because someone had told us that the cooks spit in the food when they didn't want to serve you. Other places like Bridgeman's soda fountain in downtown St. Paul, flatly refused service.*

Fairbanks and her friends staged sit-ins at Bridgeman's, although they didn't know at the time that that's what their protests were called. Finally, the manager decided that it was more profitable to serve the young people than to have eight to fifteen of them taking up stools during rush hour. But for the black teens, it was a hollow victory. "By the time we were able to eat the ice cream we had made enemies of the ones who were serving it. And since we had the old fear of people spitting in our food, we left Bridgeman's for the younger students coming behind us who had not angered the soda jerks."

The era of social protest was just beginning. In early 1960, the Twin Cities chapters of the NAACP organized protests outside dime stores in Minneapolis and St. Paul, including Woolworth's on Seventh Street. Black customers were welcome at Candyland in those days, Doug Lamb said, and in fact, Arnie had some of his best years in business in those years following the war, despite periods of social unrest and the start of devastating demolition projects downtown.

NOW SHOWING: FLIGHT TO THE SUBURBS

Downtown St. Paul, like many major cities in the late 1950s and early 1960s, was starting to look increasingly shabby and tatty as people and businesses abandoned the old downtown and moved to the suburbs. In downtown St. Paul, annual retail sales had plummeted by about $15 million between 1948 and 1954, and property values fell along with them. Federally funded urban renewal programs to help the city "sanitize, reorganize and modernize" the deteriorating downtown seemed like the answer. Once the wrecking balls and bulldozers rolled in, beautiful old buildings came down—including some of the area's most treasured movie theaters.

Since the suburbs seemed to be where the action was, Arnie decided to open a new store near his home in the first-ring St. Paul suburb of Falcon Heights. Candyland opened at Snelling and Larpenteur Avenues in 1957 and stayed in business for three years before Arnie closed it, believing that the new store was drawing too much business away from his flagship downtown store.

But downtown was about to enter a decades-long decline. In 1965, the Paramount Theater was demolished, and Seventh and Wabasha soon began to lose its vibrancy. *Pioneer Press* movie reviewer Bill Diehl wrote, "The shuttering of the Paramount removes another lure offered by the Loop, not the most exciting place to dine or seek entertainment even at the present." A year after the Paramount closed, wrecking crews demolished its lavish interior, and the Norstar, a smaller venue, opened within the space. Eventually it, too, would close.

St. Paul had long been working on revitalization plans. City thought leaders envisioned a "downtown wonderland" with modern buildings, courts, flower beds, parks and a network of skyways. Starting in 1965, new projects included a new Civic Center, Dayton's department store, the St. Paul Hilton (later Radisson) Hotel and Osborn Plaza (later Ecolab Center). But the projects were slow to be completed, and one businessman joked that downtown was the place to go if you wanted to be alone.

The postwar period in downtown St. Paul is widely lamented by those who lived through it, according to Jeffrey A. Hess and Paul Clifford Larson, authors of *St. Paul's Architecture*. First, the demolition of an old neighborhood between the state capitol and downtown forced fifteen thousand residents—potential downtown shoppers— out of the downtown area and into other areas of the city. Interstate 94 was coming through, and in the process of cutting off the capitol complex from downtown, it also obliterated the predominantly African American Rondo neighborhood just west of the capitol. With fewer potential shoppers able to live nearby, perhaps it was no wonder that downtown retail sales took a nosedive.

Making matters worse, city planners began to look at architectural treasures with scorn, declaring that these structures made downtown St. Paul look "old," "drab" and "depressing" and bemoaning the lack of "nationally acclaimed architecture in either remodeled or new structures." At that time, the height of architectural fashion meant sheathing old buildings with "clean," unadorned façades that covered up windows and lent a sleek, albeit characterless, modern look to once proud old structures. More often than not, however, it was easier to simply demolish entire blocks and start anew rather than try to rehabilitate and revitalize existing stock.

Planners excoriated the tired-looking four-block downtown retail core that included Wabasha and Seventh as a "void" and the "hole in the doughnut." Ultimately, the city and its panel of architects produced a plan to raze several blocks and redevelop the area. As Arnie Kelsey bagged up popcorn for customers, he watched out the window as some of downtown's grandest old buildings came down. The Tower Theater across the street from Candyland was among the first movie houses in the theater district to fall to the wrecking ball in the 1960s.

Streets were targeted for destruction, too, because mass transit was also undergoing change during this period. The last streetcar had stopped running in 1954, as buses proved more flexible and people fell in love with cars. In the spirit of "out with the old, in with the new," the city started tearing up the old trolley tracks. In 1955, crews removed the tracks that ran along the cobblestone on Wabasha in front of Candyland. On Seventh and Wabasha, commuting office workers and fun-seekers now spilled forth from buses out onto the downtown loop instead of streetcars.

THE HEYDAY OF THE LOOP

Understanding what "the Loop" meant to people of a certain age involves understanding what happened to Seventh Street in the postwar years. Even before the downtown reconfigurations of the 1960s and 1970s, Seventh Street's path didn't make much sense—in the Seven Corners area, Sixth Street actually crossed Seventh on its way to the Cathedral of St. Paul. The street we know today as Seventh used to be called Eighth, and at Wabasha, there was a harrowing confluence of streets: Eight and Ninth converged in what must have been a cacophony of horn-honking and fender-benders and then veered off westward toward Seven Corners and that bewildering crossing of Sixth Street. Then, as now, West Seventh Street was known as "Fort Road," going westbound from Seven Corners toward Fort Snelling.

One couldn't blame the city fathers for wanting to improve downtown St. Paul's haphazard streets, but there is considerable debate about whether the changes they wrought could be considered improvements.

"While the original sequence of numbered streets was orderly, numerous downtown reconfigurations have realigned these numbered streets so the present arrangement is incomprehensible," wrote Don Empson in *The Street Where You Live*. "Currently you can travel east on Seventh Street (which is actually Ninth Street) and run into Eighth Street…Seventh Place is a part of the previous location of Seventh Street." Today, if you look closely at the street signs on the "new" Seventh between Wabasha and Wacouta, you'll see a second, smaller street sign that reads, "Old Eighth."

In the 1960s, kids like Gary Brueggeman would ride the bus downtown on weekends or summer days with friends to goof around all day. The main bus stop was Seventh and Wabasha.

Brueggeman, a local historian and college instructor, recalled stopping at Candyland for caramel corn after getting pizza at fifteen cents a slice or ninety-nine cents a pie at Woolworth's. His mother would take him to the Fanny Farmer candy store at Seventh and St. Peter next to the Paramount. He recalled being impressed with how expensive and "classy" it was.

"But Candyland was way better than Fanny Farmer. Fanny Farmer was kind of high tone, fancy," Brueggeman said. "Bridgeman's was the other big hangout. They did malts and they made it in a metal cup, and you'd get the leftover. So you'd get like one and a half." With its location in the theater district, Candyland was a regular stop for him when he went downtown to what was still "the coolest corner" in the city. Going downtown was fun. It was an adventure, he said.

"In the 1950s, there had been changes; they lost some good buildings, but there still was a lot of really nice nineteenth-century architecture. When I was a kid, we used to love to go to the Ryan Hotel on Robert Street. Beautiful place. They used to have these fantastic buffets, prime rib. It was the greatest thing. I still can't figure out why they tore it down in 1962," he said. "Even when I was a kid, twelve years old, I didn't understand why they did it. That was supposedly progress."

The Loop was still the focal point for downtown activity and traffic, and the old Seventh was a key leg of that route. When older St. Paul residents talk about the Loop, they're remembering not only a physical traffic route but also a state of mind. Mention the Loop, and people of a certain age will regale you with stories from their high school years, as downtown St. Paul during the postwar years was a destination for teenage cruising. They beat a circular path around downtown while driving and riding in Detroit's finest chrome-trimmed, jet-finned mid-'50s muscle cars, taking in the street action and checking one another out.

Brueggeman remembered hopping in the car with older kids to drive the Loop. The scene in St. Paul in the 1960s, before the streets were redrawn and traffic rerouted, was much like the youth culture portrayed in the movie *American Graffiti*. Brueggeman worked a few miles out on West Seventh near Montreal at a drive-in that was one of many launching pads for teenage Loop cruisers. Young people would stop at the drive-in, cruise east on Seventh, come around northbound past Candyland and then head west past Mickey's Diner, White Castle and Quantrell Cadillac before heading back to the drive-in at Montreal. They'd do this over and over again on summer nights, showing off their cars. At twenty-seven cents a gallon, gas was only a couple pennies more than a bag of Arnie's caramel corn.

"The Loop was a place to cruise, and in St. Paul we cruised downtown," Brueggeman said. "The Loop was called 'the Loop' by the baby boomers riding their cars. But it was pretty silly. We'd mock the Loop later. We never met girls [while] doing the Loop. Objectively speaking, if you described what the Loop was, it was pathetic." Nevertheless, there was plenty of action downtown. Brueggeman remembered seeing *Butch Cassidy and the Sundance Kid* at one of the theaters at Seventh and Wabasha in 1969 before downtown hit its nadir. He recalled that the theater was full, people were milling about on the street and the cars were cruising the Loop.

"There was that scene. It was fun. Part of it was you looked at the street stuff happening. People coming out of the theaters. There were a couple of nightclubs: the Sherwood Forest, near St. Peter. So there were a couple of places where older people could go to nightclubs. And of course you had Bridgeman's at St. Peter and Seventh. Seemed like a lot of buses converged there. You'd wait in Bridgeman's for your bus when it was cold."

Brueggeman, like many people his age who lived through it, laments the transformation of downtown—"the beginning of the mess." Until the urban renewal efforts of the 1960s, there were a number of thriving retail businesses—from mom and pop shops like Candyland to department stores—as well as, of course, those dazzling movie theaters.

But mayors and city planners bought into ill-conceived modernization ideas that did little but bring big white elephant developments to downtown in a failed bid to compete with the suburbs and revitalize the city core, Brueggeman said. Sure, migration to the suburbs hurt cities, but Brueggeman blamed poor decisions by politicians and "cockamamie ideas" by city planners for ruining downtown and ultimately wrecking the Loop.

CHAPTER 4

The Seedy 1970s

During the 1960s and into the 1970s, the downtown that those with long memories knew and loved kept changing, and not for the better. There seemed to be little respect for the past, for the lovely old buildings. Developers shamelessly and relentlessly knocked them down seemingly without any thought, and the high cost of materials and craftsmanship make it impossible to replicate those grand structures once they're gone.

Then came the boom in skyway construction in the mid-1960s, which drew pedestrians off the city streets and indoors. The first skyway had been built in 1956—a simple, unheated and non–air conditioned affair that allowed pedestrians to get to and from the Golden Rule (later Donaldson's) department store on Eighth Street.

When city planners conceived the idea of separating pedestrian and vehicle traffic by creating a system of elevated, enclosed, climate-controlled walkways, many Twin Cities residents thought that this sounded like a good idea. But few were able to foresee what would happen to downtown life when people no longer walked or gathered on the street. Most people didn't realize that the skyways would help destroy downtown, but Arnie Kelsey suspected that drawing people up and away from city streets couldn't possibly be good for his business.

"Skyways are nice, but part of the whole downtown is walking on the street. So you had a perfect storm: skyways, [the creation of] Seventh Place and the theaters are gone where once you had the street traffic, the movie crowds," Brueggeman said. "But people would go out of their way to go to Candyland. That they survived these changes, it's unbelievable because there's just no street traffic."

Around this time, movie distributors changed the way they targeted big movie premieres, and the focus shifted to the new, modern suburban theaters. People also began flocking to new drive-in theaters, and it wasn't long before the downtown movie houses became desperate to create a profitable niche for themselves, something that couldn't be had in the suburbs. That niche turned out to be XX- and XXX-rated films, and once the downtown theaters started showing porn films, St. Paul's core became a particularly seedy, uninviting place. The Riviera Theater was one of the last holdouts—one of the last of the grand downtown movie houses to close its doors for good.

Arnie was intensely opposed to the idea that he and his wholesome business had to share the street with the X-rated movie houses, especially the Strand, which had developed into the worst of them. "He was really against everything around him," Doug Lamb said. "Everything around him was not Arnie. He didn't frequent the bars. He was very conservative. But he always made light of it. He always had a couple of jokes to tell you about what was going on."

Protesters came downtown with picket signs, decrying the demise of movies aimed at general audiences, but the movies had moved to the suburbs and weren't coming back. When the blockbuster *Jaws* opened in 1975, it chewed up screens at suburban multiplexes, not downtown. Candyland's neighbors during the '60s and '70s included a bookstore that sold adult books and magazines and a strip club. The Dayton's department store was one new bright spot in the mid- to late '60s, and by the early '70s, twelve new office buildings had sprung up. The city could boast of two and a half miles of enclosed skyways, but many empty spaces remained, including the "super hole" bounded by Wabasha on one side. Candyland no longer had much company in its formerly thriving part of downtown.

In all, the number of downtown stores plunged from more than 400 in 1963 to 160 in 1975. By the mid-1970s, city planners were faced with what would become a stubbornly persistent problem: the disappearance of downtown shopping. A chamber of commerce study in 1973 found that the new skyway system was not reinvigorating downtown St. Paul as had been envisioned. In fact, it was becoming clear that the skyways were actually diminishing downtown's vitality by emptying the streets of people.

None of this came as a surprise to Arnie. He used to chat up the mayors who came into the store over the years, Doug said, but he figured that as a small-business owner, his opinion wasn't worth much. He didn't bother getting involved with many downtown civic organizations, except for one. Despite his tendency toward cynicism, Arnie was a member of the downtown St. Paul Optimist Club. It would take optimism and more to get through the '70s.

Falling in Love with a Candy Store

Doug Lamb worked for the *St. Paul Dispatch* in the 1960s as a paperboy, and once a month, the newspaper would treat the paperboys to a movie at the Riviera, which was trying to hang on during the flight to the suburbs and the development of movie multiplexes. In the next decade, it would become hard to imagine young people going to the downtown movie district.

"The theaters were dwindling in number; they were dropping off probably one or two every two years," Doug said. "They were in decline, and of course then they got rid of the family movies and they started to be more seedy and raunchy." The Strand, which was across the street from Candyland, was the worst, and protesters picketed the theater regularly in the late 1960s. Eventually, the Strand succumbed, closing its doors for good in the early '70s.

Candyland had some rough times itself in the 1970s. Employees pilfered money from the cash register; one was even suspected of breaking into the store. So Arnie was relieved when he found a trustworthy high school kid to work for him when he needed the extra help. Doug was seventeen years old and worked after school at Candyland starting at 4:00 p.m. At the time, the store opened at 10:00 a.m. and stayed open until 10:00 p.m., Sunday through Thursday, and 11:00 p.m. on Fridays and Saturdays to serve the movie crowd.

There were still some downtown shoppers who would come into the store, but shopping had been dying off throughout the 1960s. Office workers were good customers—St. Paul Fire and Marine (later the St. Paul Companies and Travelers) was the biggest employer downtown in the 1970s. Burlington Northern Railroad, located about ten blocks away in Lowertown, was another big employer, and those workers visited Candyland regularly. "We got to know them quite well," Doug said. "At BN, they got an hour, hour and a half lunch breaks, so they had all the time in the world."

Doug Lamb started out waiting on customers, keeping the store clean and managing the business at night. Arnie had one employee working at night on weeknights and two people on Friday and Saturday nights. He paid $2.45 per hour, which was a princely sum for a high school kid at that time. Doug also worked at Applebaum's department store, but it only paid him $1.90, so when given the choice, he worked at Candyland and looked forward to the day when the boss would entrust him with the store's most closely guarded secret: the caramel corn recipe.

"At night, he would never teach you how to make caramel corn. You had to work during the day to make caramel corn, and he only did it if you worked during the day with him," Doug recalled. "The only other person who knew how to make caramel corn was the person who worked Saturdays and Sundays, and they were told not to teach anybody else. He was afraid somebody would steal the recipe."

When he did finally teach Doug to make caramel corn, Arnie had him sign an agreement promising not to disclose the recipe to anyone. The same went for Arnie's homemade fudge recipe, which was the original one used at the store for decades: sugar, milk, unsweetened chocolate, butter, vanilla, corn syrup and walnuts.

Doug continued:

> *When I started, he had some of everything we have now. Back then, he couldn't have chocolates in the summertime, so the whole chocolate case was filled up with hard candies…He used to make popcorn balls in the '50s, and then he quit, and we brought them back. He always made fudge. Peanut brittles. He used to make divinity—egg whites, sugar, corn syrup—and you cook the sugar and corn syrup together, then pour it into a mixer and slowly pour egg whites into it, and it becomes real light like nougat. Not like a taffy. Lighter than fudge. But he quit making that, too. He felt he wasn't making money at it. Divinity is a lot of work. To make five pounds it might take three hours of work, and he was probably only getting $1 a pound back then.*

When Doug started working in 1974, he staffed the store by himself every night except weekend nights. If he brought in $100 a night from 5:00 p.m. to 10:00 p.m. or 11:00 p.m., Arnie considered it a good night and loved to see $100 in the nightly take. "I wouldn't do anything special," Doug says. "If I was still cleaning at 10:30 p.m., I'd say, 'Come on in.'"

Teenagers still drove the Loop on Friday and Saturday nights well into the 1970s. There were no one-way streets at that time, but there was a well-worn route around downtown and certain landmarks. On Eighth Street, today's Seventh, were landmarks such as Mickey's Diner, the White Castle across from where the Xcel Energy Center is now and the Quantrell Cadillac dealership near Seven Corners. Candyland benefitted greatly from being located in the heart of the Loop.

Doug continued:

> *People would cruise around Seventh, Eighth, go around about seven blocks. There wasn't a lot on Eighth Street; it was more just a space to park. A lot of the buildings had burned down. There was the bus depot there that took up half a block. Eighth*

Street wasn't really a hot street. There was a bowling alley on it; you'd cruise by the bowling alley. There was J&M Bar, Miller's Bar. At night, your big motorcars came out—the Chevys with the chrome. Everybody did the Loop. The suburbs didn't have that. So Friday, Saturday nights were the busiest nights of the week at the store. And then Sundays were always busy. They didn't come down to drive the Loop, but Sunday night there was wrestling night at the old Williams arena.

Unlike today, the popcorn bags were small—about eight ounces. When Doug went to work at 5:00 p.m., he was tasked with packaging up dozens of bags of popcorn for the grab-and-go crowd, the teens who wanted nothing more than to get back to their cars. "You had to bag up the caramel corn so when they came in you just handed them the caramel corn, and they're off. Friday, Saturday nights were big nights. You'd come in to work and you had forty, fifty small bags on the table, and you had your eight-ounce bags down below on a counter, and you had to fill that up because Arnie would tell you it's going to be a busy night because of the Loop. He had to have fudge slices, bags of peanuts in the shell and caramel corn. They'd pull up out front and get their bag and go around the Loop again."

The public's snack tastes were quite different in the 1970s. Peanuts in the shell were wildly popular, and the store still makes use of a fifty-gallon barrel that used to be filled to the brim with peanuts in the shell. Doug remembered lugging heavy gunnysack bags of peanuts—as well as one-hundred-pound bags of brown sugar—down the stairs. He'd empty the peanuts into the barrel and then bag them up for the Loop cruisers, lining a shelf with ready-to-go peanuts and caramel corn. "They didn't want to wait for you to bag it up," he says. "They'd run in, run out. Everybody was in a hurry. I always think back, why were they in a hurry? They had no place to go. They'd go in a circle."

On Sundays, Brenda Weber would come down from the suburbs to pitch in and hang out with her boyfriend, Doug. "It was a cultural experience," she joked, remembering the shabby atmosphere of downtown St. Paul in those years. "You had places like a strip club right next door to you and a liquor store right on the other side of that. But there were still department stores. There was Dayton's; there was Donaldson's. All the shopping was on the street."

Laurie Johnson worked for Arnie from 1974 to 1979 and helped out at the St. Paul store over the Christmas 2013 season just for fun. Johnson worked from 10:00 a.m. to 5:00 p.m. six days a week in the '70s, and she remembered that there was a certain rhythm to daily life at Candyland. Arnie was a mild-mannered and undemanding boss.

"It was just Arnie and me during the day, and he had one or two boys come on at night for the night shift," Johnson recalled.

> *Sometimes I would work at night—that was fun. You would crank the radio up and play tunes of the '70s, or if it was during the day, Arnie and I listened to classical music. I would start my day by filling the candy cases and filling any empty bins that needed refreshing. We made caramel corn throughout the day, popcorn throughout the day.*
>
> *People would kind of drift in and out. I would be pretty much busy restocking things. Once a week, it was my job to change the display in the window, which everybody hated to do because you had to climb up into the caramel corn bin in the window and reach over, and it was awkward; it was not fun. Arnie had little dishes of candy out, and they had to be rotated depending on the season. Sometimes the windows would steam up, and the candies would just get nasty and they'd have to be thrown out.*

Lunchtime was busy as the regulars from the downtown office buildings came in for popcorn. The Strand Theater was still operating when she worked at Candyland, and there was parking on either side of it because some of the old buildings lining the east side of Wabasha had been torn down. Johnson used to park there for fifty cents per day. The Riviera was still open, too. "People would come in and get their popcorn and smuggle it in. The theater had signs up saying you couldn't bring your own popcorn in, but people did if they got small enough bags. Weekend nights were busy."

Until 1979, air conditioning in the old building was a touchy, iffy system, and Arnie wound up throwing away a lot of chocolate when the system broke down. Sometimes he had to store candy at his home in Roseville, and Doug remembered helping him bring chocolates to his house. From there, the goodies would often go to Arnie's church for after-service coffee-hour treats.

Beryl Kelsey was still working at the store one day a week in the early '70s, and Doug recalled that she and Arnie had distinctly different communication styles with their employees—something of a good cop/bad cop management approach. "If something was wrong, she'd let you know it," he says. "Arnie might beat around the bush to let you know it. Very quiet guy. His wife was very assertive. If there was a problem, the next day Arnie would say, 'Well, Beryl says…'"

PEEPHOLES AND GEARSHIFT POPPERS

Before going to work for Arnie, Doug's brother, Greg, worked for their father's firm in the Endicott building, running down to the basement to have blueprints made and ogling the treasures in the window of the coin shop on the first floor.

As a suburban kid, he wasn't much of a St. Paulite until he started working for Candyland in the mid-'70s. Like other kids his age, he and his friends sometimes went downtown to race around Seventh Street, cruising the Loop down the main drag and up around Mickey's Diner on Eighth and around St. Peter Street. That was his introduction to St. Paul, and like many baby boomers attached to the freedom of their cars, they rarely bothered to stop, get out of the car and hang out downtown, although he did sometimes buy nickel licorice ropes and go to the Riviera to catch a movie.

If you were looking for adventure, you could always find fascinating little nooks and crannies to explore in downtown St. Paul's eccentric old buildings. The first Candyland space in the Riviera building had a narrow hallway alongside a wall leading to the upstairs, which had a low half-room with a slanted ceiling—a sort of loft—where Arnie kept all his stock. Doug and Greg and Arnie's other young employees had to haul cases of candy up the steps for storage and then fetch them down from up there when needed.

Greg recalled:

> It was such a short space, you'd kind of be half-cocked on your knees walking in and out. You could actually be up there and look down into the store through kind of a split in the ceiling about two inches wide. You could watch what was happening down in the store if you wanted to. I don't know if that was on purpose in case a boss wanted to hang out there and watch the activity down below, but I remember that you'd kind of look down the slanted roofline before it hit the wall coming up to it and there'd be a couple of spaces, cracks, an inch or two wide, where it just viewed right down into the store. And the old store had the craziest, tiniest little crappy bathroom, like you'd find in a camper.

Arnie had an older version of the drum-style popcorn-popping machine Candyland uses today. The old popper had mechanical gearshift levers, much like a car with a manual transmission, according to Greg:

> It had a forward speed, a neutral gear and a reverse gear. And you would have to move a few levers to put it into gears. You could jam it, but it was pretty easily repaired. Kind of a cool machine to run. It was kind of a Model T of a popcorn machine.
>
> Now they have a motor, and you just hit a switch and move the switch back and forth on these newer machines. The whole drum is cantilevered on a large shaft about two feet long, and if the bearing wears out, it starts clunking. It was fun to operate because it required a little bit of skill. You had to be careful with it, you know. Break the machine and you're out of business. That's still true to this day. That's the beauty of having all these stores now. If a machine goes down, the other stores can support them. Arnie didn't have that option.

Greg began working part time at night for Arnie after his brother started working at Candyland and remembers the late 1970s and early 1980s as being the low ebb for both downtown St. Paul and the store. Downtown shopping was dead, and there was no nightlife to speak of—other than a few dive bars in the immediate area. There were higher-class saloons a few blocks west and south near the St. Paul Hotel, but in general it was "pretty dumpy," Greg said. When Doug and Greg began working at Candyland, many of the theaters were still in operation, but just barely.

Dubious Downtown Characters

Those few businesses that remained in the neighborhood were run by a few of St. Paul's most notorious characters. Victor Costello had his newsstand on the northwest corner of Seventh and Wabasha in front of the lobby entrance to the St. Francis Hotel, and former Chicago Bears player Al Baisi was co-owner of Alary's, which was then a strip bar two doors down from Candyland. The sweet shop's immediate neighbor was a liquor store. Liquor and candy always do well during times of economic recession or depression, said Greg of Candyland's knack for survival.

"A big deal on Saturday nights was Victor on the corner selling Saturday night newspapers, and a lot of those customers would make a trip to Candyland, too," he said. Costello's newsstand was a little wooden shack that resembled an outhouse. "Literally with Victor it *was* his outhouse. That's a pretty grimy story in itself. He would have a few of the dirty magazines in circulation at that time to sell his customers."

Costello had been in trouble in the '50s and '60s for minor offenses such as gambling and selling liquor without a license at his downtown market. But as a fixture on Seventh and Wabasha, he was a beloved character who waved at passersby and seemed to know everybody who frequented downtown. Customers stood in long lines to buy their newspapers from Costello and the Weisberg brothers, Solly and Max, who were infamous for their bookmaking activities. Max Weisberg was a mentally impaired numbers savant who ran afoul of the law a few times, especially after his brother died. The judicial system somehow never got around to jailing him. Nicknamed "Maxie Flowers," Weisberg sold cut flowers in addition to newspapers.

"The flower guy, Arnie didn't like him too well," Laurie Johnson said. "In the summertime, Arnie would have the door open to get some fresh air in if it wasn't a day for air conditioning, and [as] this fellow would walk by, he would always holler in, 'Kelsey's hot nuts!' And Arnie's face would just turn all red."

Johnson said that the prostitutes and strippers were none too good-looking in the daylight, and Arnie often had some snide comments to make about them. The strippers worked at Alary's, and Greg knew both the cofounder Al Baisi Sr. and his son, Al "Junior," the present owner. "I knew the woman who would escort Al Sr. into the joint every night because he was blind, and she would walk him down the block. He'd come into Candyland, and she'd come into Candyland and buy him a little something and take it up to the bar for him."

Vagrants and street characters would mingle with customers who were simply aged and infirm, those for whom a trip to Candyland might have been a way to revisit memories of downtown during the 1930s and '40s. "We used to have a person who'd come into the store and buy sponge candy or fudge or something and have us cut some fudge for them. But she was so old and frail, we'd bring out the one and only stool we had in the store for her to sit on in the corner so she could rest," Greg said. "We serve customers for decades, and we'd see them old, then we don't see them anymore. I've seen a couple decades of families with their kids and grandkids."

The cycle continues to repeat itself. Now that he has been at the Minneapolis store for thirty years, he experiences similar relationships there. "Customers would come in all the time and call me 'kid.' Older customers would. A few of them now, to this day, they still call me 'kid.' Some things never change."

A New Home

Doug Lamb worked for Arnie part time until 1978, which was a particularly difficult year for the older man. Beryl died in 1978, and then Arnie got word that the Riviera was going to be torn down. The landlord had given him no notice, and since his store was in the same building as the Riviera, he would have to move.

Arnie scrambled to find a new spot, and he got a verbal agreement for a place one block south, on Wabasha between Seventh and Sixth. That owner wound up giving the space to a smoke shop called Tobacco Road. Arnie was furious, but he soon learned that 435 Wabasha in the old St. Francis Hotel building was available, the space in which Candyland is now located, and that ultimately turned out to be a better spot.

So, in 1979, Arnie finally got his chance to move closer to the corner. By the time he moved the store, Candyland's end of the block was a wasteland of boarded-up storefronts, and he felt that potential customers would not walk the extra one hundred feet from Seventh and Wabasha to his door. Seventh was still a desirable street to be on or at least had sentimental meaning, and Arnie still wanted to be there—a dream that got passed along to the Lambs and that remains unfulfilled to this day.

Walgreens had long occupied the southwest corner of Seventh and Wabasha, and it still operates there now. Retailers had come and gone on the northwest corner since the St. Francis Hotel (later the Capri Hotel) closed, and in 1979, Musicland was the tenant there. Next to Musicland was a clothing store, and next to the clothing store was Candyland's new space.

The new store was a huge improvement over the old one: bigger, newer and cleaner. The space included a nice big sink in which to work, compared to the tiny sink at the old store. There was a nice storage space; you no longer had to lug boxes of candy upstairs.

"Arnie figured if he got closer to the corner, it would be better for his business because he could capture some of these office people," Doug said. "He figured he was losing money because the business people didn't want to take an extra three minutes to walk X amount

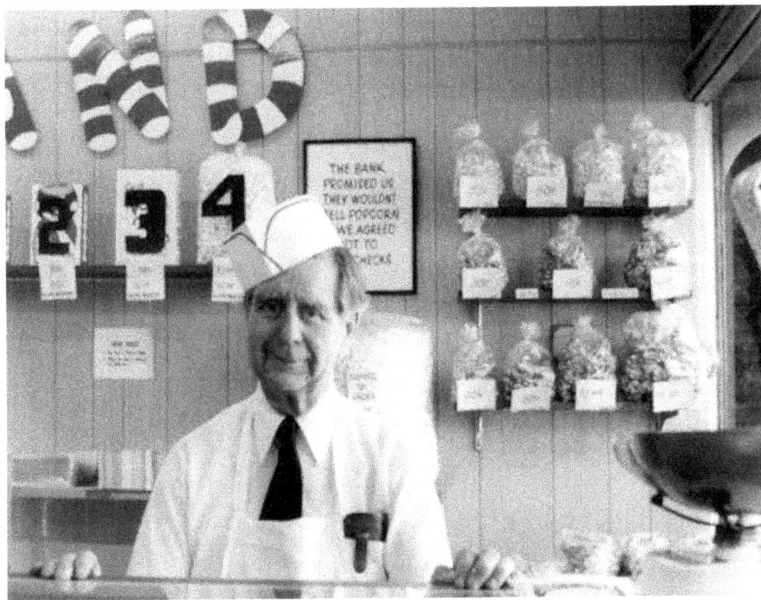

Many St. Paul downtowners knew Arnie Kelsey as the "sad-faced candy man." He is pictured here in the old store in about 1978 or 1979.

of feet because they were in a hurry. It didn't really happen. He didn't really capture them. Instead, it got worse. People left. The retailers left."

Once again, however, Candyland wound up being the unlikely beneficiary of downtown's misfortune when a major competitor, the Fanny Farmer sweet shop on Seventh opposite Musicland, closed. So now when downtowners needed a chocolate fix, Candyland was the default option in the Seventh and Wabasha area, although some chocolate lovers might have made a trip to Dayton's department store for its famous Frango mints.

"When I started working for Arnie in 1974, the buildings were beautiful still, everything was full—there were no vacancies. I came across a picture when he moved in 1979 to 435 Wabasha, and the picture is terrible," Doug said. "On the east side of us, the stores are vacant; there's no rhyme or reason to the signage. Our building was restored in 1991–92; the building owners got some money from the city, and they brought it back to its original shape.

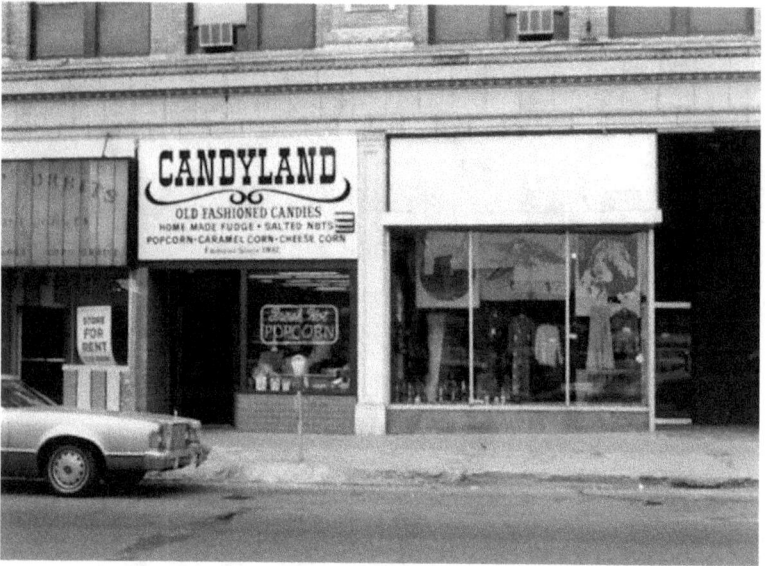

In 1979, Kelsey moved the store to its present location, deepening Candyland's commitment to downtown St. Paul as other small shops closed.

Otherwise, over the years, they took brick and they covered up brick with wood and made it an ugly building. And it's actually a gorgeous building now."

At one time, the cavernous basement that ran underneath the St. Francis Hotel building extended from the Orpheum Theatre all the way to Candyland. If you go down the store's basement steps and walk straight ahead, you come to a wall that used to be a makeshift door accessing the entire block underground.

"That's one spooky place," Greg said. "Doug got robbed a few times from kids exploring down there—finding that doorway and coming up into Candyland. So they walled it off. We used to go down there and walk around those rooms down there. It was just dusty and dirty. There were really no rats or anything because there was no food anymore."

Indeed, the block was quite empty when Arnie moved to the new space. Besides the newsstand, Alary's and the liquor store, there was also the Hello Dolly bar next to the Orpheum—another dive bar.

Other than the apartments in the old hotel, it was nearly deserted in that little corner of the city, except for the bustling vice trade. But St. Paul was about to embark, again, on ambitious plans to clean up and revitalize downtown. This time, the plans would mean the end of some of the city's most elegant old structures, including the movie houses that had managed to survive the initial postwar cleanup efforts.

When the Riviera Theater complex was razed in the mid-1980s, Greg took a melancholy walk down to the rubble pile on the corner of Eighth and Wabasha. He grabbed a large green-and-yellow chunk—a piece of the terra-cotta molding from the outside of the once proud theater.

CHAPTER 5

The End of the Loop and a New Beginning

S t. Paul's business community and elected officials had been trying for years to figure out how to get shoppers back onto the streets again—particularly on Seventh Street, where they hoped to create a magnet for shoppers.

The big idea for the now-empty space on the east side of Wabasha was Town Square, a development that included office towers, a three-level retail mall, a hotel and a light-filled indoor park. As part of the Town Square development, Seventh Street was to be closed to traffic and made into a brick-paved pedestrian mall extending one block from St. Peter on the west to Wabasha on the east. It would be called Seventh Place Mall. Ironically, the city's true town square would be killed off by a development whose name would never live up to the original.

The end of the Loop as a teen cruising destination and the end of the Seventh and Wabasha corner as downtown's main gathering spot came in 1980 and 1981 as the long-planned and long-delayed Town Square project was completed amid much fanfare. The newspapers and local television stations hyped it. For a few years, Town Square and the adjoining World Trade Center did draw shoppers and businesses, and Candyland enjoyed a bump in the number of visitors to the store. But by the 1990s, Town Square and the World Trade

Center had become troubled projects. Stores inside the mall opened up, struggled to lure customers and eventually closed. Gangs were drawn to the indoor park, whose nooks and crannies were difficult for police to patrol. The Cafesjian Carousel and its beautifully painted antique horses came to the park, languished and galloped away to a better home near Como Zoo and Conservatory.

The old Seventh and Wabasha movie district was unrecognizable and seemingly beyond rehabilitation. The Orpheum Theatre, which had hung on during the 1970s, finally closed for good after Seventh Place opened.

"Seventh Place opened in 1980. What a mess," said Gary Brueggeman, echoing the thoughts of Doug and Brenda Lamb. Like other cities, St. Paul tried to reinvent itself but wound up ruining its city core. "A lot of cities wrecked their downtowns by making malls. It was a phase: 'We're going to make a mall.' They tore down buildings, they literally closed down the street and they made a building right where the street was."

The project turned into yet another white elephant, Brueggeman noted. The hotel and park eventually closed. Everything that was promised went bust. The mammoth Town Square project involved closing off Seventh Street, which meant rerouting traffic to Eighth Street and renaming it Seventh. Today, the street maps show Sixth Street, Seventh Place, Seventh Street and Ninth Street.

"The damage they did is incalculable. They destroyed Seventh Street," Brueggeman said. "All these big projects they had petered out. Downtown St. Paul is a hodgepodge of different administrations starting over, having different plans. Where is the Main Street of downtown St. Paul? There isn't one."

When the city closed off Seventh Street, that's when downtown became a ghost town, Doug noted. "Nobody liked downtown anymore. They took away the Loop. People were just leaving left and right."

It was a long haul out of the gutter for all of downtown St. Paul, Greg Lamb said, and there are still huge pockets of inactivity or flat areas around downtown. "There's bad space layout, bad city planning. They should have never ripped out Seventh Street and stuck that mall smack dab there. It just ruined traffic flow all around downtown," he added. "And I wish they would have saved some of the old buildings. In retrospect, now they would. They'd save them and revamp them, and they'd be cool places to live. Can't go back in time, though."

Despite the street reorganization and the closure of Seventh, 1980 was actually a good year for Candyland's business. It enjoyed a temporary uptick in customer traffic as the curious came downtown to check out the new indoor park and shops. Doug believes that the store's prosperity was largely due to Arnie shortening store hours and reducing staff. By this time, he was getting tired. He was aging, he had lost his wife and after forty-three years selling popcorn and sweets, he was losing interest in the business. Brenda Lamb said that the business was in retrenchment mode during the 1980s. Candyland was doing the same thing it had always done and wasn't expanding or trying anything new.

"Now you had someone who was pretty much done; he didn't want to do more. He wanted to do less and less," she said. "So he cut his hours down. He closed on Sundays. It was a downslide for him and for the store, too."

His young employee, meanwhile, was taking architectural drafting courses part time at Dakota County Technical College in Rosemount and Inver Hills Community College. Doug's father had been a mechanical engineer who worked with architects and draftsmen in the Pioneer Endicott Building, and his son figured that he'd follow a similar path. He remembered staying up until 5:00 a.m. finishing a project whose design incorporated glass block. "I got really crucified on the project," he recalled. "They thought I was crazy because they said that was something that was not used any more and won't be again. Of course, now you see that all the time in a lot of high-end homes and a lot of places. So that was the end of that."

It was just as well. Lamb didn't know what he was going to do next, but he did know that he liked to work on his own. He was still working at Candyland on call, and his brother was working for Arnie regularly. One day, Greg called to say that Arnie was thinking of selling the store to one of the full-time employees, since none of Arnie's grown children was interested in taking over the store. But

Arnie Kelsey mixes caramel corn in his store in 1974.

Arnie was troubled about how the employee was going to finance the deal. The employee was going to buy Candyland with money borrowed from news shack owner Victor Costello, and Arnie would have none of that. He didn't like the prospect of Costello getting his nose in the business.

"I thought that was pretty funny," Greg said. "Yeah, that's just what we needed: Victor with part ownership of Candyland. He would have run it into the ground. I'm sure Arnie and Victor had some history; I mean they worked on that same block for decades. In the era Arnie grew up in, which was the Depression, it wasn't unusual to cohabitate with these denizens—the 'crooked timber of humanity,' as Cormac McCarthy put it in one of his books."

With encouragement from his brother, Doug started putting some serious thought into buying the business. Brenda remembered that Doug's coursework in drafting didn't seem to be sitting well with him, although he did continue to enjoy the hours he spent at Candyland.

"Oh, Doug loved the business," she said. "He loved the environment of this little retail store. He loved the people around it. He liked the people, he liked what he was doing and he thought the product was the best. He thought it was a great product, and he thought that this was really what he wanted to do. And Arnie knew that he was the one meant for this business. You can always tell with employees, the ones that take the care to do things. The honest ones. [Doug] would always make sure things were done right."

Looking back, there was no apparent upside, nothing particularly positive, about the Seventh and Wabasha area when the Lambs bought the store. Other retailers were either leaving or already gone, and the city wanted a new look.

"There was nothing good about it. They're connecting all these buildings with skyways, and nobody's going to come outside anymore and you're outside. Nobody can get to you by the skyway," Doug said.

> *The Loop's gone, totally gone. They're getting rid of the bars; they don't want any of these bars anymore. They want to clean up the city. They don't want naughty bookstores, but those were good customers of ours, too. Theaters, gone. The theaters were desperate; they needed money, so they went to the X-rated movies and the city wanted them out of there…We weren't thinking about that. We were not thinking about that at all. We just loved candy and popcorn…and how can you not make it in business with candy and popcorn? What were we thinking? We were young. I wanted to work for myself, and I told that to Arnie. He had a good product.*

Candyland Changes Hands

Doug Lamb bought the business in 1981 for about $100,000. Arnie had been paying himself about $33,000 at the time. He stayed on part time afterward, coming in at 10:00 a.m. and staying until 2:00 p.m. It was time for him to call it quits, but it was also hard for him to separate, Brenda said. "It's hard to leave something you've done for forty-three years, and he wanted to make sure we were doing it right. There were a few times he just looked at me like, 'Are you sure you want to do that?' He didn't say 'No, don't do that.' He'd just give me the look."

Arnie also had his longtime buddies downtown—one sold hearing aids, and another owned a clothing store. "He'd go out to lunch with them once in a while," Doug recalled. "He wanted to keep in touch with these people. He liked the guy with the clothing store; he was a character. Nate's Clothing. That was his buddy, and he always talked about him, and they all ended up retiring about the same time. And when Nate left, Arnie realized, 'Hey, my friends are gone. I'm going.' So he left. Or Brenda forced him out," Doug said with a laugh.

"He stayed with us two years, part time, and then I told him he had to leave. It wasn't quite like that, but it was time. You could tell," Brenda added. "I know that he felt comfortable because at times he'd work with me and didn't seem to be aware that I was standing there. And I was the one working with him because Doug still worked another job. Doug felt that this was not going to be enough income, and he worked an overnight job until he was sure everything ran smooth and we were able to support ourselves. He didn't know if this business would be able to do it."

At the time, Arnie only opened the St. Paul store on weekdays, so the Lambs brought back evening and Sunday hours. "It took time to build it, too. It wasn't like it was instant good business," Brenda said. "You have to be patient and you have to build your business, and that's what the downfall is with a lot of businesses. They have no patience, and they go, 'Oh, there's no business. I'm not going to open these hours.' Of course, you have to have funds behind you, too. Some people lose money, and they just can't afford it."

Brenda was twenty-one, and the couple had two children: Vanessa, born in 1976, and Trisha, born in 1978, the year they bought the store. Their sons, Brandon and Jordan, were born in 1987 and 1992, respectively. Doug was not at the store much, so Arnie was training Brenda.

He was very subtle if he didn't like what I was doing. He'd make very dry, sarcastic jokes. I just remember if there was anything

I was doing that he didn't approve of, he was very sarcastic. He didn't say it just like, "You're wrong." He never would say that.

I remember one time a salesman came in and wanted me to try a product that wasn't real butter. And [Arnie] just looked at me and said, "You going to try that?" I mean it was a lot cheaper. I said, "I don't know. It's pretty good." And he just looked at me and said, "You'll be sorry." So right then I go, "Forget it. Nope." And that was the last time I ever thought of changing any of the good-quality products.

Unlike today, there were no phone orders back then. Sales came by way of walk-in traffic only. It was a simple business. There wasn't even a dedicated business phone line in the store—just a pay phone in the customer area. In those pre-cellphone years, the phone company paid businesses to put pay phones in their stores. Calls cost a dime. If somebody called the store, you had to go across to the customer side and answer it.

BRANCHING OUT

Once they learned the ropes from Arnie and got comfortable running a business, the Lambs decided to expand. In the early 1980s, they opened two new locations in downtown Minneapolis: one on Seventh Street off Hennepin and one inside the old Lasalle Court off Nicollet and Eighth. They opened a location at the Mall of America in 1993, becoming one of the first tenants at the megamall.

Using the basic knowledge they'd picked up from Arnie, they taught themselves more about the candy business. They started dipping their own chocolates and making their own fudge using Arnie's old recipe. But it was also time to start playing with some different ideas. They tried new recipes and new combinations of treats, learning by trial and error. They made their own Victorian brittle and toffee bars by taking a basic recipe and improvising on

Brenda Lamb tends to the peanut brittle. *Photo by author.*

Opposite, top: Butter toffee popcorn with cashews, almonds and pecans was given the name "Flavo Crunch" to honor the store's history. *Photo by author.*

Opposite, bottom: Candyland's "Chicago Mix"—plain, cheese and caramel corn.

it. They started making caramel for snappers and apples, something that hadn't been done at the store since the 1950s.

They came up with new creations such as butter toffee popcorn with cashews, almonds and pecans and called it Flavo Crunch in honor of the store's roots as Flavo Korn. They took trips to snack conventions in Chicago and absorbed information and ideas. One of Brenda Lamb's most lucrative brainstorms—Chicago Mix popcorn, on which they own the trademark—came after such a trip in 1988.

"It was a Sunday and I was working, and it was like one hundred degrees outside. And one hundred degrees is not our business. We don't have the ice cream. So I just took a little bucket and mixed some popcorn together. In Chicago, they just do cheese and caramel. But their regular popcorn and seasoned popcorn is just horrendous. Ours is very good. And ours in our downtown store was probably our top seller because in a downtown area people eat it every day. It wasn't a treat, it was part of their diet."

So on a whim, Brenda tried mixing Candyland's three popular popcorn varieties together—plain, cheese and caramel—and slapped a label on the bags: "Chicago Mix."

"I couldn't even believe the first day how much I sold. I bagged up some bags and put them on the counter, and the rest is history. It's been incredible. It's actually gone worldwide. Not by me, but by people stealing the name. We've had huge companies that have stolen the name. In 1992, the trademark was finished, so we own the trademark and we have since then. But there are some very large companies that have stolen the name, and a little company like me can't fight that, unfortunately."

At first, the Lambs sent cease-and-desist letters whenever they caught another company using the name "Chicago Mix." Typically, the offending entity would apologize, offer to change the name of their product, their lawyers would call the Lambs' lawyers and that was the end of it. Large snack companies continue to flout the trademark and use the Lambs' "Chicago Mix" name, but far-flung popcorn lovers who have tasted Candyland's specialty mix will go to great lengths to get it. Today, the store ships its now-famous Chicago Mix to devoted popcorn fanatics around the world who have discovered the old shop on Wabasha Street.

"Candyland went through a low spell, but they also sprang back real quick," Greg said. "Doug and Brenda made vast improvements right off the bat. Spruced the place up, started making things that Arnie didn't make. Started buying other candies for the next generation of kids. Without those changes, it wouldn't have sprang back the way it did. They brought new life to an old business, and it was worth it."

CHAPTER 6

Downtown

A Development Drama in Several Acts

The city's efforts to lure people back to what was now Seventh Place included an attempt in 1984 to inject charm by paving the street with brick, putting up a picturesque arch and placing planters along the way. The charm offensive failed to draw people or businesses, although there were a few bright spots: a farmers' market began operating on the mall during the summer months, and the Actor's Theater renovated the old Norstar Theater (a smaller venue located in the old Paramount Theater space) into a premier performing space, thanks to funding from the city.

For a few years, Garrison Keillor's *A Prairie Home Companion* radio variety show operated out of the old Orpheum Theatre, which had been shuttered since 1982, before moving to the renovated World Theater space—rechristened the Fitzgerald Theater—on Wabasha and Exchange Street.

The Lambs have absorbed Arnie's longtime obsession with occupying the northwest corner spot on Wabasha and Seventh Place. For one thing, the space is bigger; also, corner exposure is simply good for attracting customers. But a big part of the appeal was admittedly sentimental: The Lambs inherited a legacy business, and they have a profound sense of respect for Candyland's history and longevity on Wabasha and the old Seventh.

Candyland has been in its present location on Wabasha Street since 1979. The brick-paved area down the street once was Seventh Street, the most popular intersection in downtown St. Paul. It is now known as Seventh Place Mall and is closed to traffic.

By the 1980s and '90s, it wasn't an easy corner to love anymore. Where once there were theaters, bars, restaurants and throngs of people, Seventh Place Mall was now a dead-end empty block bookended by the St. Paul Companies tower at one end and the underutilized Town Square/World Trade Center development at the other. Even the colorful characters—the bookies, the strippers, the grizzled girlie-magazine peddlers—were gone. Seventh Place was "a wind-swept alley, devoid of color and action and people," wrote the *Star Tribune*'s Joe Kimball in 1990. "Empty storefronts now stand watch over the once-festive strip. Passersby don't stop to shop or look; there's nothing to attract their attention."

After only a few years, the Actor's Theater closed, leaving the block nearly deserted, although Kimball noted that city and business leaders continued to harbor ambitious plans to make the block come alive with outdoor cafés and boutique shops again. The city movers and shakers envisioned a return to the days when Seventh was where people headed when they came downtown to visit the theaters, have a drink at the Hello Dolly and the Whiskey-a-Go-Go or eat at the Haberdashery—when office workers, teens hanging out downtown and ladies on shopping trips waited for a bus at Bridgeman's. It was a nice dream, but it would be a tall order to recapture the magic of a fabled thoroughfare on this street that no longer went through and no longer had much fare to offer.

Regardless, the lifeless Seventh Place still managed to stir up passions. In 1991, Doug and Brenda Lamb threatened to leave downtown St. Paul after their landlord reneged on a preliminary deal to rent the spot on the northwest corner now occupied by Bruegger's Bagel Bakery in the Seventh Place Building (the old St. Francis Hotel). In early September 1991, the Lambs signed a letter of intent with Landmark Management Corporation to lease the 1,200 square feet of space.

But after a major announcement that the Children's Museum of Minnesota was going to be redeveloping the old Riviera Theater space, Landmark suddenly did an about-face and signed a new letter of intent with Bruegger's. The president of the leasing company told the news media that he felt the decision would benefit the area in general and Candyland in particular. The Lambs, who had been excitedly drawing up plans for an expanded shop and candy kitchen, begged to differ. They felt betrayed and bitterly disappointed. Doug lamented to the *Pioneer Press* that similar deals in Minneapolis were honored—why not in St. Paul? Despite the hard feelings, the Lambs decided to stay in their location at 435 Wabasha. This was not the last time the Lambs would become embroiled in the debate over the fate of Seventh Place.

In 1999, the St. Paul Companies insurance firm bought the Seventh Place Residence apartments, composed of 130 low-income units in the historic St. Francis Hotel building and the Palace/Orpheum Theatre, for $1.6 million with the intention of leveling the Seventh Place Mall block for an expansion. Emotions around the issue were high: News stories from that year describe the dismissal of three preservation commission members who favored historic designation for the buildings, marches by housing advocates protesting the St. Paul Companies' plans and angry vows by the owners of the Original Coney Island never to sell. Organizations that opposed the demolition of Seventh Place buildings supported the Lambs' offer.

Eventually, the St. Paul Companies pulled out of the deal. In May 1999, the Lambs offered the St. Paul Port Authority, which owned the Palace/Orpheum and the Seventh Place apartments at the time, $1.6 million for the property. With preservationists on their side, the Lambs hoped to save Seventh Place's historic buildings, maintain the affordable apartments and use their know-how and connections to attract new retail businesses to the troubled block. Doug Lamb told the newspapers that he intended to lease out the rest of the retail space on Seventh Place Mall, including some eight thousand square feet on Wabasha for a grocery store, and figure out a new, creative use for the theater.

But in July of that year, the Lambs got word that the St. Paul Port Authority had approved the $1.85 million sale of the Seventh Place Residence to a St. Paul apartment and investment management company, Kelly Brothers. Kelly said it planned to maintain affordable, moderately priced apartments at the site, but the Lambs and area preservationists feared that the company might turn around in a few years and sell the buildings to other developers that would demolish the building and displace its residents. Their fears were unfounded; today, the apartments above the Palace/Orpheum, Bruegger's and Candyland are home to a new generation of downtown dwellers.

FAMILIES AND KIDS RETURN TO DOWNTOWN

Feeling burned by the port authority and once again denied that cherished spot on the corner, the Lambs licked their wounds by focusing on their new Mall of America and Minneapolis stores. Then came their new neighbor in downtown St. Paul, and with it came perhaps the best thing a candy store could wish for: families and kids.

The Minnesota Children's Museum opened up in the old Riviera building in 1995 after having outgrown its home in Bandana Square. The museum was just the shot in the arm that Candyland's long-neglected part of downtown needed. One book described the museum site in the 1990s as being situated "at the northern edge of the historic theater district, its immediate predecessors were a derelict movie theater, a seedy residence hotel, and a hodgepodge of commercial buildings stripped of their historic fronts...The edge of the property wrapping around Wabasha Street butted up against a post–World War I multiple-use building housing the St. Francis Hotel and a sequence of street-level stores," including Candyland.

The new, light-splashed three-story Children's Museum cost $16.1 million to build, and its glass front looked out onto Seventh Street (old Eighth). An estimated 400,000 people would visit the museum annually, according to projections at the time. Brenda Lamb was quoted in the *Star Tribune* in September 1995 about the museum's opening sounding more cautious than optimistic. She worried about whether people would find parking and be able to walk across Wabasha, which was torn up at the time for a sewer project. "We're looking forward to it," she said of the new Children's Museum. "But St. Paul has a lot of things that don't pan out."

Indeed, museum visitors didn't venture outside the building at first. It took two years and a desperate move by Brenda—placing a giant inflatable slushie balloon outside her store—to lure those first moms, dads and grandparents to the treat shop a few doors down. Today, Candyland has a partnership with the museum and regards the museum as a great neighbor. Parents toting little ones frequently follow their noses to Candyland after visiting the museum.

Not everyone is enamored of Candyland's sensory delights, however. After ten years, the Lambs were kicked out of the Mall of America in 2003 when a leasing agent said their products stank and refused to extend their lease. The Lambs told the *Star Tribune* that they had waited for months to get their lease renewal papers, but mall officials kept putting them off. "We finally got a call back; he said they'd decided not to renew our lease," Brenda Lamb told the newspaper. "We asked why and he said, 'Because of your smell, you stink.' We were shocked."

With all of the tourists and the families visiting the mall's amusement park, Candyland naturally did a strong business at the mall, but the Lambs had no choice but to pack up and reallocate their employees to the downtown Minneapolis stores.

GOODBYE TO THE "SAD-FACED CANDY MAN"

Arnie still stopped in at the St. Paul store now and then during the late 1980s and 1990s. He had remarried in 1982, and he and his second wife, Helen, spent much of their retirement traveling and wintering at their condominium in Phoenix. Even between visits, his presence was still felt at the shop that he ran for four decades. For years, a wood carving of Arnie's face, crafted by his daughter Judi, hung above the caramel corn cookers. A December 1997 *Star Tribune* story about Candyland's legacy described Arnie at age eighty-two dropping in at the shop after hip surgery.

"The business starts getting in your blood after 40 years," he told the newspaper, confessing to having grabbed a chocolate-covered peanut or two back when he ran the store. As a result, he once weighed more than 200 pounds before cutting back on the snacking and trimming down to 170.

People called him the "sad-faced candy man," Doug recalled of his former employer and friend. "It's almost like he didn't like people, but you have to like people to be in business," he said. "He made it through the ups and downs, so he must have done something right. He wasn't happy or didn't seem happy. I just thought he was a quiet guy. It's funny because when he went into the nursing home, he wrote a joke book. Pretty corny. Jokes he had written down all his life, and he composed a book out of it."

Arnie and Arvin were still buddies and even wound up at the same Roseville nursing home. Arvin was at one end of the building, and Arnie was at the other end, Doug recalled. "Arnie would say, 'Hey, want to go see Arvin?' And I'd say, 'Why, is he close?' 'Oh yeah, you don't have to go outside; just walk way to the other end of the building.' That's the last time I saw Arvin."

Arnie died in 2004 at age eighty-eight and Arvin in 2006 at age ninety.

CHAPTER 7

Morning at Candyland

The gas burners are already fired up under the copper pots and inside the six-foot-high industrial air popper on a Monday morning before the store opens to the public. It's time to make the day's first batch of caramel corn.

There's clarified butter warming on a hot plate and several cups of brown sugar in a stainless steel bowl on the scale. You make a well in the middle of the brown sugar, and with a large, heavy metal spoon, you scoop the gummy, clear corn syrup from a white bucket, twirling the spoon to wrap the ropey substance around the spoon. You then let the thick syrup ooze into the well in the brown sugar bowl until the scale registers the correct weight.

"We have a certain brown sugar that we use. I pay a lot more for it than I have to because I want to use that brown sugar. It will change our product if I use something different," Brenda Lamb said. "My sugar company kept bringing us samples of other sugars to try, but no. The good brown sugar we use is just different. Cooks different—everything's different about it. They brought me another sample of something because at the time they didn't think we'd be able to get that good brown sugar, and sure enough, it wasn't bad, but it was definitely sweeter. It didn't have the rich caramel flavor to it." It's the molasses that lends that unmistakable flavor.

Brenda Lamb measures brown sugar before mixing a batch of caramel corn.
Photo by author.

You transfer the brown sugar and corn syrup mixture to one of
the copper pots, where it cooks and bubbles for a few minutes in
the rounded, well-seasoned bottom. Next into the pot goes a hunk
of butter—you don't stir it in, you simply allow it to cook down

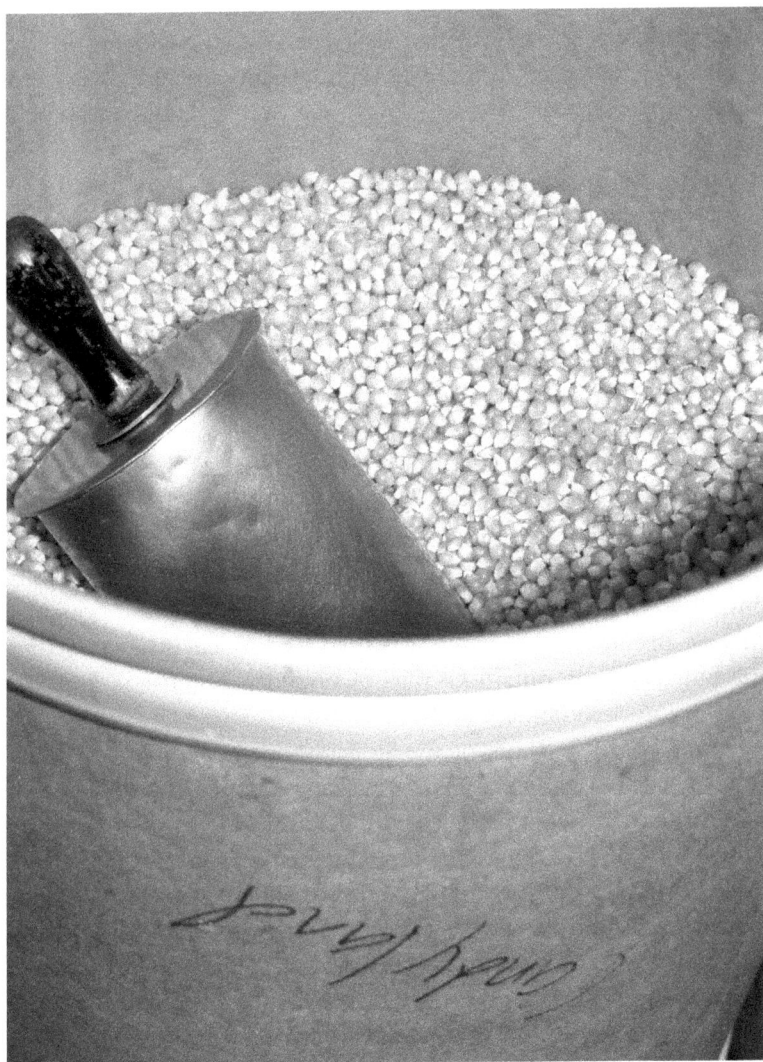

Candyland buys popcorn in fifty-pound containers. *Photo by author.*

with the brown sugar and corn syrup mixture. That distinctive Candyland olfactory siren song begins to fill the air. While the contents of the copper pot bubble, you start the popper spinning. The spinning barrel has a kidney-shaped opening in the side. Using a tubular scoop, you quickly toss the kernels into the opening. Inside the drum is metal mesh that will separate unpopped kernels from the large, domed "mushroom" popcorn, a variety that holds up best for caramel corn.

As the drum spins and the kernels heat, you think about the simple physics of popcorn. Each kernel contains a small drop of water stored inside a circle of soft starch. Popcorn needs between 13.5 percent and 14 percent moisture in order to pop. The soft starch is surrounded by the kernel's hard outer surface. As the kernel heats up, the water begins to expand. At a temperature of about 212 degrees, the water turns into steam and changes the starch inside each kernel into a superhot gelatinous substance. When the kernel reaches about 347 degrees and the pressure inside the grain reaches 135 pounds per square inch, the hull bursts open. As it explodes, steam inside the kernel is released. The soft starch inside the popcorn becomes inflated and spills out, cooling immediately and forming into fluffy white popcorn shapes. Brenda said that she was surprised to learn recently that the hull is a fairly nutritious part of popcorn because it contains the most antioxidants.

Popped corn spills out of the kidney-shaped opening and into a stainless steel holding tray. You transfer the popcorn into a bucket and turn your attention back to the boiling contents of the copper pot. Now you toss in a spoonful of baking soda to thicken the mixture slightly and stir vigorously until blended. The color lightens from a deep and somewhat translucent brown to a lovely, foamy caramel. Then you wait for the concoction to start smoking—if you don't wait, the caramel corn will be too chewy. It's ready when the caramel is smoking and almost smells burnt.

When it's time, you transfer the popped corn into the copper pot. Using a large wooden paddle, you must quickly stir and toss the caramel corn while stabilizing the heavy pot against your hip. This takes practice; the pot doesn't want to stay against your side while you work. You slide the paddle down the sides and across the bottom of the pot, tossing the caramel corn quickly and continuously to coat each piece. The metal pitcher of clarified butter sits nearby, and you drizzle some over the mass of caramel corn.

Brenda Lamb uses a large wooden paddle to mix caramel corn. *Photo by author.*

Once the popcorn is thoroughly coated, you grab the pot by its wood handles and carry it to a stainless steel trough by the store window, where you hoist the heavy pot and dump the contents out onto the surface—being careful to keep your distance from the hot lower section of the pot. Using a large metal scoop or a gloved hand, you break up the clumps and toss the caramel corn for a few more minutes.

Making caramel corn Candyland-style isn't as easy as Brenda Lamb makes it look, and new employees aren't put on caramel corn duty until they've absorbed some basic store knowledge first. It takes a significant amount of muscle to lift the pots and even to stir the caramel corn, and Brenda has the muscles and—as her husband points out—the arthritic hands to show for it. An energetic morning person, she's constantly in motion, moving easily from making caramel corn to scoring trays of Victorian peanut brittle. Scoring the brittle will make it easier to break into neat little rectangles that will get dipped in chocolate and sprinkled with toffee bits.

A $3.5 MILLION–A–YEAR BUSINESS

Brenda Lamb mixes about 32 pounds of fudge every few days using Arnie's old recipe. She buys popcorn in 50-pound bags—the large yellow variety for plain and buttered, mushroom for caramel corn and cheese corn—and pops about 200 pounds of popcorn every day (about 400 pounds a day during the holidays) at the St. Paul store alone. It works out to about thirty-six tons of popcorn a year. The store also buys sugar and brown sugar in 50-pound bags, and Candyland uses about 125,000 pounds per year. The store goes through a staggering 20,000 pounds of chocolate, 40,000 pounds of cheddar cheese and more than 200,000 pounds of butter per year.

Chicago Mix popcorn and chocolate pecan "snappers" are the store's most popular items. Among the nostalgic candy that Candyland carries are Jujubes, rock candy, Mary Janes, licorice black pipes and Bonomo Turkish taffy. When the Lambs bought the store in 1981, it generated about $100,000 in annual revenue. Today, the Candyland stores employ fifty-seven people and generate $3.5 million per year.

Brenda Lamb's workday usually begins at 5:00 a.m. at home on the computer, answering e-mails. She drives into the city at

Raspberry, hazelnut and carrot cake truffles.

about 7:00 a.m. to get the store ready to open. Since the store is open until 10:00 p.m., she wants to get in and see what happened the night before. If her young employees didn't do their jobs properly, she finishes what they were doing or cleans up after them. Sometimes she makes toffee or some other buttery treat before the store opens and the popper starts running. If the floor needs mopping or the sidewalk out front needs shoveling or sweeping, she does that, too.

"Just call me the janitor," she joked. "Get the computer going again, open up e-mails again, taking orders, seeing what the big orders are for the day. It's kind of continuous, nonstop. Making sure the pick-up orders are organized and done on time when the customers come in."

Before opening, she also delivers products to the gift shops in Minnesota state office buildings that are run by a program for the blind. Doug floats around among the stores, fixing machinery that no one else knows how to fix. But he often thinks of getting behind

Gas-fired popcorn popper. *Photo by author.*

the counter again to wait on customers, just because it's what he has always liked doing.

Doug's brother and sister and the couple's two daughters and two sons team up to run the four Candyland stores. In 2012, they opened a shop on the main drag in historic downtown Stillwater. Brandon Lamb runs the Stillwater store and has inherited his parents' passion for the business. While showing a visitor around, he proudly rattles off all of the items that are made within his shop: the popcorn, homemade fudge and hand-dipped chocolates.

"There will be times where if St. Paul has a large order, we'll take care of it; we'll help each other out," he said. But mostly each store produces its own goods for its own customers. Brandon Lamb said that he and his siblings learned how to make candy over time, and each has his or her particular interest or specialty. "If we feel like you have the knack to cook popcorn and the desire, then you can. If not, that's fine."

Every morning at the store is spent doing a bit of prep. They don't have to wake up at 3:00 a.m. like bakers or work overnight because Candyland's homemade items are quick to make throughout the day. In a popcorn and chocolate shop, typically you can get a fresh batch of everything within thirty to forty minutes, Brandon said.

The popcorn equipment is "the heart of the store," he noted. Because they don't pop any of their popcorn in oil, the pieces are larger and more consistent. The hot-air poppers used at Candyland are a unique design; only one company makes them. "You throw the popcorn in the same way it comes out," he says. "It's designed with a wire inside there that gets smaller as it gets farther down; the seeds are able to sit down in there and sit over the open flame. So they're kind of constantly tumbling, getting consistently hot. And when they pop, the kernels will grab onto the wire and come right back out."

The copper kettles are also important pieces of equipment. The Lambs prefer cooking over gas flames, not electric burners, and copper conducts heat well and evenly. Besides cooking their specialty popcorn in these kettles, they also cook fudge, brittles and other products.

PARADISE: THE CHOCOLATE ROOM

The chocolate room contains one "enrober" for milk chocolate and one for dark. Next to the enrober is a bowl for tempering the chocolate—a chunk of chocolate is placed into the back of the bowl, and it slowly melts into the basin. A constant spinning motion over heat will churn the chocolate until it reaches a smooth consistency. A chain then draws the chocolate up into a chute, and the person making the chocolates—the "dipper"—can control the thickness of the chocolate coating.

The belt turns, allowing the dipper to evenly coat items with the tempered chocolate. It's a slower, miniature version of the conveyor belt that gave Lucy and Ethel so much trouble in the iconic *I Love Lucy* chocolate factory episode. The motion of the mesh belt shakes excess chocolate off, and the treats are then transferred to a tray and arranged on tall cooling racks.

Chocolates are dipped throughout the day on an as-needed basis. In St. Paul, there's someone in the chocolate room all day, every day, because stock will run low very quickly at the busy flagship store. Because the Stillwater location is relatively new, there's a little less demand. Brandon Lamb is still trying to grow the Stillwater store, so for now he has someone come in to dip chocolates just one day a week.

"In St. Paul, you probably can go there any morning, and there's somebody dipping during store hours. It's a separate room, so we like being able for our customers to visually be able to see us making products. You can watch, and that makes it more interesting," he said. "Dipping chocolates is very time-consuming. Chocolate is a very temperamental thing; it's a substance where the temperature of the room makes a difference. The humidity…these kinds of things will affect it. So whoever is doing the chocolates really has to know what they're doing as far as what the temperature of the chocolate is based on those temperatures that day. There are a lot of variables that play into it."

Similarly, with homemade caramel, brittle and English toffee, understanding the cooking temperatures and consistency takes time and experience. Candyland's fudge recipe is pretty much the

Chocolate dipper Rose Thorson creates a batch of milk chocolate–covered nut clusters. *Photo by author.*

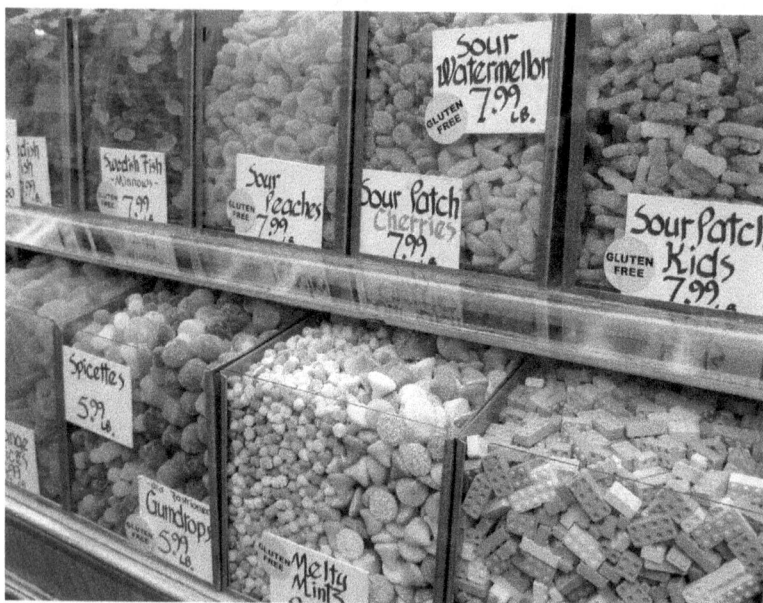

Changing with the times: the store offers a range of gluten-free candies. *Photo by author.*

Opposite: Christmastime goodies at Candyland.

same basic 1930s-style fudge that Arnie made and that the Lambs' mother used to make. Greg has made a niche for himself making the blond penuche (or panucci) fudge sold at the Minneapolis stores.

"It's brown sugar fudge that tastes like the frosting on a German chocolate cake without the coconut," he explained. "With fudge, if you overcook it, it gets harder and whiter on top. It gets kind of a film of cloudiness. If you undercook it, they don't set up and get as firm as you want, and they can be soupy. So if you're going to do one or the other, I'd rather overcook it. It'll still taste great, just has a little cloudiness on top, but it's firm so you can cut it well."

As time has passed, Candyland's products have changed along with public taste and trends. Today, the store labels the bins containing candies that are gluten-free for customers who need those products. Dark chocolate's antioxidant properties have made

it a huge seller—especially dark chocolate and almonds, which are believed to be heart-healthy—and sweet-savory sea salt is a popular ingredient. But customers also ask for nostalgia candy that they remember from decades ago. The Lambs call Candyland a "generational" store, one that attracts people who visited when they were young and now come toting children and grandchildren.

Unlike the old days, Candyland's walk-in business makes up only a fraction of its overall sales today. The downtown St. Paul store deals with Internet order fulfillment and shipping all day long, with UPS and U.S. Postal Service pickups twice a day. "All of this going on in a little old store," marveled Brenda Lamb, who also oversees deliveries.

Trucks can't park at the downtown store, so deliveries go to a kitchen/warehouse near the Minnesota state capitol complex. During the Christmas holiday season, the busiest time of the year, one of the Lambs' daughters runs that kitchen to fill corporate orders that roll in. The kitchen has a popper and cookers to handle the overflow for the St. Paul store's business and the large corporate orders. There is space at the site to store the one thousand to five thousand pounds of candy the Lambs order at a time from about twenty different companies. They order direct, never from distributors. If you buy from a middleman, you don't know how long that case of candy has been sitting around, Doug said.

Online and phone orders from businesses for corporate events, employee recognition ceremonies and parties are a big part of Candyland's modern business. Weddings, showers, school events, formal dances, carnivals, bat and bar mitzvahs and class reunions— these are just a few of the special occasions for which Candyland provides the goodies. The store also offers extravaganzas such as its "popcorn buffet," with bags and bowls full of Candyland's signature popcorn varieties. Similarly, its candy buffet is a beautifully arrayed display of 250 different candy and chocolate items for special events. Candy centerpieces, chocolate gems in team colors, popcorn tins in a variety of sizes for parties or holiday giving are also available for special gatherings.

It's a far cry from the days when the store's stock was determined by the status of the building's air conditioning unit.

CHAPTER 8

Kids in a Candy Shop

Candyland is a textbook example of a family-run business. Doug Lamb's brother, Greg, and sister, Julie, have worked at the Minneapolis stores for years, and the Lambs' four grown children divide their time among the four stores. Greg is an artist who once created watercolor paintings for family and friends and now does all of the old-fashioned hand-lettering on the cards identifying the candies in each clear bin. Julie Stewart, who started working at Candyland when she was sixteen, manages the Minneapolis stores and handles a variety of duties there with help from Doug and Brenda's kids.

When Doug and Brenda bought the business in 1981, their daughter Vanessa was five years old and Trisha was about three. Their children grew up amid the din of industrial popcorn poppers and the scent of sugar and chocolate. Each of her children had a different level of tolerance for going to work at the candy store with mom when they were babies, and Brenda said that daughter Trisha was particularly easy to take along. Brenda would take her to the store on Sundays when the girl was just a toddler.

"Many Sundays, she would come with me. It would be her choice. I'd ask her, 'You want to come with mom or stay with dad?'

From left: Vanessa (Lamb) McDonald, Trisha (Lamb) Quaale, Brenda Lamb, Doug Lamb, Jordan Lamb, Julie (Lamb) Stewart, Brandon Lamb and Gregory Lamb. Greg, Julie and Doug are siblings; Vanessa, Trisha, Jordan and Brandon are Brenda's and Doug's grown children. *Photo by author.*

And she would come with me. She was the type of child where if I told her not to touch something, she wouldn't touch it. And she was quite tall for her age, so people thought she was a little older than three. We had this old steel bucket in our store, and she would stand on it and do little things to help out."

With the help of the bucket, she could see over the counter and interact with customers, who were charmed by the little curly-haired girl dressed up in a tiny apron and hat uniform like the other employees.

Brenda knew from a young age that she never wanted to work for other people, and she set her sights on working with dogs. Ever since she was fifteen years old, she had dreamed of becoming a dog groomer. Once married, she planned to run her own dog-grooming business out of the home in which she and Doug would live. "Thank goodness Doug decided this [Candyland] was the business for us," she says now.

Family Business Rule No. 1: Give One Another Space

Taking young children to work is part of the package when you run your own business, and after buying Candyland, the Lambs were careful not to jump into it blindly. Doug hung on to his day job, with its health benefits, for a year after they bought the business, until they felt that Candyland could generate a stable enough income to support their family. During that year, Doug would work nights, and Brenda worked some of the day shifts, alternating schedules so that they'd each have time with the children at home.

Once they determined that Candyland could indeed provide a stable income, Doug quit his office job to devote his time to the business. But apparently there is such as a thing as too much togetherness for couples who work that closely together. Brenda is a self-described workaholic who admits to being independent and headstrong. Doug is considerably more laid-back. It wasn't long after they bought Candyland before Brenda started calling it her store.

"He quit his job after a year, and then he started to work more in my store, and I couldn't handle it—I couldn't stand him," she said with a laugh. "So we decided to open a new store in Minneapolis in 1983. It took us not too long before I decided, 'We can't work together,' so he decided it was time to maybe branch out."

When their son Brandon was born in 1987, she took one week off and went back to work toting the baby. It helped that he slept constantly—even through feedings. Since he slept so much, she parked him in the back room at the St. Paul store in a portable bassinet while she took care of the store. After a few months, family and friends took over the childcare.

As the kids grew up, they inevitably gravitated toward working at the store, doing chores and odd jobs. "They didn't really wait on people, of course," Brenda Lamb said. "Eventually, everything just came to them. And I'd say, 'Hey do this little project, do this little thing.' Brandon wanted to wait on people so bad that when he was eleven, he took one of my applications and filled it out and gave it to me. He wanted to be hired to wait on people because he's

Doug and Brenda Lamb. *Photo by author.*

very personable, and that's what he really wanted to do. With him, the height was there, too, so there was no problem with being able to reach the counter, so he started to wait on people when he was eleven. Trisha was even younger than that."

All of the Lambs' children went into the family business after high school, Brandon and Jordan after attending community college for a few years. Each has his or her own particular interest. Vanessa McDonald enjoys working with chocolate and is Candyland's primary chocolate dipper. Unlike her mother, who puts in long hours at work and at home, Vanessa has made it clear that she has no interest in keeping the long hours of a shopkeeper like her mother. Trisha Quaale floats among the three Minneapolis and St. Paul stores, wherever she's needed most, opening, supervising employees and waiting on customers, according to Brenda:

> *Trisha does everything. She'll report back to me if she sees something that should be corrected, and hopefully she tries to work with it as much as she can. Her niche is customer service. She's excellent, really good with people. She runs my store on Saturday, which is the busiest day of the week now. I'm comfortable walking away from that store on the busiest day of the week because I know she's there. Otherwise, I'd be working that day, and I don't want to. I do sometimes, but just fill-in, especially if she's gone. Then I'm there. But being that it's the busiest day of the week, I don't worry about it so much. But the phone is always in my pocket. It's always good to have communication if there's a problem. I'm there for them.*

Jordan, the youngest, had no interest in the business as a youngster and wasn't particularly outgoing, and Brenda said that to this day, she is surprised that he is involved with the stores. She and Doug always encouraged their kids to pursue whatever interests they wanted to pursue, and they thought it would be best for Jordan to take some college courses, research various career options and figure out his true calling. "But then he just fell into the business because I think it was just easy for him to be there," she said, adding that he's also personable and very good at customer service. "You give them the opportunity to do other things, and if they don't care for it, you don't force them. That's always what our thoughts were for bringing up children. We always said, 'Okay, we want you to try this.'"

She hopes that Jordan will take on the niche of running Candyland's Internet business, but she won't let him do it unless she knows he's going to do it right "because that can destroy you in your Internet business if it's not done right." She'd love for him to go back to school to learn web design so that he could take the website in-house and turn it into an e-commerce site. Brenda Lamb is convinced that this could be Jordan's unique contribution, his specialty, in the business, as well as a way to take fuller control of an aspect of the business that until now has been hired out.

RULE No. 2: THERE'S ONLY ONE BOSS

Ideally, Brenda would like for each of her kids to have his or her own particular way of contributing to the business. However, someone has to take the lead with a family business, and right now that leader is Brenda Lamb. Inevitably there are conflicts, especially between Brenda and Brandon—he also wants to take a leadership role in the family business. "We butt heads a bit," she said. "He'd like to push me out; he thinks he can do it on his own, but he can't. I said I'm not ready to go yet. But he likes to press my buttons sometimes, and I have to explain to him that I'm still in control—you aren't."

Brandon always knew that he wanted to be involved in Candyland and wanted to be successful at it, she said. "And he is. He is the one who stepped it up in the business. He's the one that really is aggressive, he's the one who brings in ideas, he's the one that changes things [and] he's the one that makes adjustments. The other ones kind of just go with the flow. And that's the difference."

Brenda and Doug say that of all of their children, Brandon is the one who brings ideas to the table for new products. Some of the ideas sounded good in theory but didn't work out so well in practice, such as a chocolate with rice crisps and ganache that would have been too perishable to be practical. However, not all of Brenda's ideas work out as well as Chicago Mix, either. One year, she was convinced that cinnamon popcorn would be a winner for the holidays, and although the reddish, Christmas-y looking snack didn't bomb, it didn't sell as well as expected. And Tabasco Jelly Belly jellybeans, hotter than Hot Tamales, also didn't sell well.

Brandon is the one who wants to expand the business, although not necessarily with more stores. He has experienced firsthand with the Stillwater store how much work it takes to run a brick-and-mortar shop and deal with the disruption to one's personal life when an employee calls in sick and you have to go to work on your day off. Brenda often reminds him that he can't do everything himself, but she admits that it's also hard for her to delegate responsibility to non-family.

Rule No. 3: Manage Conflict. Learn to Delegate

The Lambs are always mindful about maintaining Candyland's old-fashioned appeal, and they believe that adding too many stores would mean losing some of the charm that comes from having passionate, committed family members at the helm. They are cautious about bringing non-family employees into the inner circle, although Brenda said that they have started to bring one or two employees closer and give them more responsibility out of necessity. Right now, they have just enough family to run four stores. Any more stores, and they'd have to look outside of the family for managers.

"Then you're not going to have family there, and there's no one that can run a family business like family," she said. "You will never be able to replace someone who's actually a co-owner or who is into the business, brought up in the business—the person has a heart and soul into the business. There's no way." She finds it very difficult to let go enough to delegate responsibilities to non-family members. There's a constant push-pull between wanting to let go and wanting to maintain control.

"When you start a business where you have very few employees and you're used to doing everything yourself, and you know the business and you know that you can do a better job than anyone else, you tend to start doing it yourself," she said. "But you have to start letting go, you have to delegate, or else you'll never have any free time. You have to. And sometimes you can do it, and sometimes they fail you or sometimes they do a great job and you're so pleased. But if it's a non-family member, it's still not like having a family member. There's no comparison."

Doug's sister, Julie, said that she never planned on making Candyland her life's work, but thirty-plus years later, she's still a key part of the operation in her role as a manager of the Minneapolis stores. She makes candy—toffee, Victorian brittle, peanut brittle and coconut brittle—and handles some duties that she doesn't find nearly as enjoyable, such as hiring, firing and scheduling employees.

"I stay there and make sure everything gets done," she said. "I'm in both Minneapolis stores. I'm in one store two days a week and one store three days. It's a lot of work. Doug and Brenda have done really well for themselves. It took a lot of hard work for them to do that. It's very physical. It's fun. Candy-making is a lot of work."

There are pros and cons to working with family. Julie noted that they don't always see eye to eye and that sometimes family members take things more personally than they should. Brenda agreed, adding that besides the work of the business, it takes work to keep the family relationships healthy.

"A lot of people say, 'Never have your family work for you.' And that is sometimes true," Brenda said. "It depends on the personalities. And we butt heads. All of us have done it. But you have to separate the business from your family and personal life. And sometimes you don't succeed. But you have to work at that, that this is not a personal thing—this is a business decision, and this is how this matter is being treated.

"When you boil it down, the word is *respect*. You have to respect each other. But unfortunately things can get out of control. But I think all in all, through all these years, with my sister-in-law and brother-in-law working with us, I think it has been a positive over a negative."

Being able to retreat to different stores certainly helps give feuding family members a little space to get over a spat. And

Brenda noted that unlike families who have feuds that might result in a years-long estrangement, that can't happen when your colleagues are your relatives.

"That can't happen with us unless someone quits. We haven't had that happen yet," she said. "But we get mad at each other, and because we're around each other, it kind of works out. We realize the anger isn't worth it. We have to work it out because we have to talk; we have to communicate. But there might be a twenty-four-hour period where we might not speak. That's kind of normal."

Although it seems counterintuitive, running a family business can take a lot of time away from family. Family time especially suffers during holidays, Brenda said, because that's when the stores are busiest. When the kids were young, the Lambs did take family vacations, but trips are out of the question now, so they try to coordinate short, in-town gatherings: concerts, birthday dinners out and the like. For Jordan's twenty-first birthday, Doug and Brenda took Jordan and Brandon to Las Vegas, but it was just for two and a half days.

Besides having weekend plans spoiled when an employee calls in sick, there are the occasional emergencies that every business owner has to sort out. Recently, the Lambs got a midnight phone call after a would-be thief broke into the St. Paul store. The burglar had professional tools and got in the front door in mere seconds, but he couldn't get the electronic cash register open. The security tape shows him bashing it onto the floor when the store's alarm went off. There was nothing in the register, so he fled. Doug had to hop out of bed and go downtown to talk to the police and make a report.

RULE NO. 4: CELEBRATE SUCCESS

The upside of being involved in a family business? "We see each other all the time, we work together, we have lots to talk about," Brenda said. "The conversation is about everything, the everyday life there, the funny things a customer might do or something that

Display shelves filled with varieties of fresh popcorn. *Photo by author.*

might happen. It gives great conversation. Or, the downside is people say, 'Oh, that's all you talk about is work.' Well, that's our life, and we talk about other things, but the business does take a major part of everything."

Generally, enjoying the benefits of the business together, watching the business grow together and reflecting on what they've accomplished is a great reward. Greg said that it makes him happy to know that Candyland has not only survived but has also grown into a thriving local business. Because of that, Doug and Brenda are able to give back more to the community, Greg noted. Every year, they get besieged with more requests to provide products for various Twin Cities charitable events, such as school and church fundraisers. Candyland has a partnership with the Shrine Circus in which the store provides popcorn for sale so that the Shriners don't have to deal with making it.

Arnie would be pleased with these sorts of efforts, Greg said. After Arnie died, his second wife, Helen, told the Lambs that he often expressed gratitude about what they'd done with the business and pleasure that it was growing and flourishing instead of deteriorating.

In the wrong hands, it would have been easy to destroy the business, Brenda Lamb said. "[Arnie] always had been very happy that he sold us the business and was very comfortable with what we'd done. We've always kept the name and the quality of the business. So I think that's very important. And also bringing up your children in the business—it's important that they understand what level to keep it at. Keep it basic, keep it old-fashioned. You can grow with it but don't change the basics of the business because it's going to take away from it, and people are going to know that it's different."

CHAPTER 9

Seventh Place and Wabasha

There's no shortage of ideas for injecting new life into downtown St. Paul, although a lot of the attention lately has been directed toward the hip Lowertown on the opposite end of downtown from the Seventh and Wabasha area. Young people and empty-nesters are taking up residence in renovated historic buildings in Lowertown and at the architecturally significant Pioneer-Endicott building. The St. Paul Saints minor-league baseball team is getting a new stadium near the Lowertown farmers' market. The Union Depot train station renovation is complete, and bus and rail transit is moving through the station again. The president even stopped there to make a speech.

Now the Wabasha Street area seems poised to get some overdue attention. The Dayton's department store that butts up next to Wells Fargo Place begat Marshall's, Marshall's begat Macy's and Macy's closed in 2013, leaving downtown without a department store for the first time in decades but presenting an opportunity for creative repurposing. When MinnPost.com wrote about the Macy's closing, a few commenters waxed nostalgic for the old Seventh Street. One said that the St. Paul Port Authority should level Wells Fargo Place and Macy's and reopen and reconnect the old Seventh. Sweet memories die hard.

Brenda Lamb is involved with a civic group called Wabasha Partners, whose mission is to support the revitalization of Wabasha and see it reach its full potential as a downtown destination again. Among the issues on which the group took a position was a proposal to route a bike path through the downtown Loop. Although drawing bicyclists to the Loop would generally be a positive for the city, the group opposed that idea because it might mean losing more precious parking spaces. St. Paul's downtown streets are narrow, and parking would likely have to be removed in order to accommodate bike trails.

Meanwhile, the area continues to undergo a slow and steady transformation. Candyland's next-door neighbor to the north, Rivertown Market grocery, is undergoing its first ownership change in forty years with the retirement of longtime owners Gene and Harriet Will. The Wills sold the business in early 2014 to a couple that intend to continue it as a mom and pop market, despite the opening of a new Lund's grocery store downtown.

Fine dining at restaurants such as Meritage, the St. Paul Grill, Pazzaluna and Kincaid's is helping draw people to Candyland's neighborhood again, and less expensive food and drink can be had at the brewpub Great Waters Brewing Company and Wild Tymes on Seventh Place. The renowned Dakota jazz club is taking over the Artists' Quarter space on Seventh Place in the Hamm Building, much to the delight of jazz enthusiasts on the St. Paul side of the river. And the Park Square Theatre continues to offer quality plays in an intimate setting inside the Hamm Building on the Seventh Place Mall.

Nearby, the Minnesota Children's Museum is planning a $28 million expansion that will increase space by 50 percent and give passersby a glimpse into the four floors of fun inside through glass walls. Town Square and the World Trade Center didn't pan out as envisioned, but the office tower, rechristened Wells Fargo Place, is now home to government offices whose workers are good Candyland customers.

One vestige of the old Seventh Street theater district is getting some attention again thanks to the efforts of a highly placed booster: St. Paul mayor Chris Coleman. Coleman was a city councilman

Lucy is a popular companion for photo ops.

in 1999 when then-mayor Norm Coleman and downtown business interests sought to take the wrecking ball to the Palace/Orpheum Theatre and the adjoining St. Francis Hotel as part of the planned St. Paul Companies expansion. Preservationists were elated that

Coleman and the Historic Preservation Commission prevailed and won historical designation for the buildings at Seventh Place and Wabasha. Today, tenants of the apartments in the old St. Francis include students who attend the McNally Smith College of Music a few blocks north of Seventh Place and Wabasha.

The Palace/Orpheum's last tenant was the Brave New Workshop comedy troupe, which held shows in the lobby until calling it quits in 2005. Now the theater is being targeted for a $12 million restoration that Coleman hopes will make it a centerpiece for an arts and culture district similar to that in Austin, Texas. The Palace would be a "Goldilocks" concert hall—not too small and not too big— offering a 3,000-seat showcase for contemporary pop music shows. Although it originally seated 3,000, a redesign in the 1940s cut the seating to 1,400, and it was converted to the RKO Orpheum movie theater in 1947. The theater was home to *A Prairie Home Companion* temporarily from 1982 to 1984.

A permanent use for the theater has proven elusive. "These historic buildings are not easy to get back online," Coleman told the *Star Tribune*. "But you have to do it [or else] let it sit and deteriorate more."

AN ENCORE FOR DOWNTOWN MOVIES?

Not everyone agrees that a concert venue is the best use for the Palace. Art gallery owner Bill Hosko and many downtown residents favor returning the space to its former glory as a movie theater, arguing that downtown needs to have a movie house again. The downtown business and residents group Capitol River Downtown voted in March 2014 to ask the city to investigate movies as part of the renovation process. St. Paul hasn't had a downtown movie theater since the Galtier Plaza theater closed in 1999.

Whether it would host concerts or movies, preservationists hope that the Palace could be restored and reopened in time to mark its 100th anniversary, and it would mark a milestone in the attempt to make downtown St. Paul a destination for entertainment again. State Representative Alice Hausman commented to the *Star Tribune* that people have changed their habits over time, and "whereas they used to go downtown to shop, they now go to be entertained." Coleman said that adding vibrancy to Seventh Place would make it easier to fill vacant buildings and storefronts such as the vacant Macy's department store.

A renaissance of entertainment in the old theater district would be good news for Candyland, although the business has shown an uncanny ability to survive despite the comings and goings in downtown St. Paul. There was an effort to rejuvenate the old Palace/Orpheum as a concert venue before, and that effort failed, Greg noted. Candyland is doing great without an operational Palace Theatre, he said, because now St. Paul has a lot more going for it: great restaurants, theaters, museums and sporting events such as March Madness tournaments at the Xcel Energy Center—all of these are well promoted and bring potential customers around for Candyland.

And while Greg believes that St. Paul should have done more to save the inexpensive stores where people used to shop, such as Woolworth's, he likes the idea that unique little retailers such as Heimie's Haberdashery menswear are still hanging in there despite the ebb and flow of office tenants over the years.

"We've lost lots of regulars from offices, and that's from companies leaving, buyouts," Brenda said. "I don't think the office work environment is what it was twenty years ago. We've lost a lot. But lots more families come downtown. The Children's Museum, the Science Museum, they try to have family events around, which is good. Our business is still always growing. After all these years, we do have a following, and people go out of their way to come into town to the store."

Candyland is not only a destination for the average Twin Cities resident, but it also attracts high-profile athletes and celebrities. Britney Spears came in to one of the Minneapolis stores alone once during a concert tour stop, although Doug didn't know who she was until someone clued him in later. The late Twins star Kirby Puckett was a regular customer whom Brenda Lamb described as a down-to-earth guy who always wore a gray sweatshirt that didn't look like it had seen the inside of a washing machine very often. Puckett usually ordered a large cheese corn with butter—"a handful is probably five hundred calories," Brenda noted—and was always accompanied by a bodyguard.

Actor Richard Burton, comedian Red Skelton, former Minnesota Viking and current Minnesota Supreme Court judge Alan Page, ex-Viking Carl Eller, former Twins outfielder Dave Winfield and writer/entertainer Garrison Keillor all have been Candyland customers. At the other end of the spectrum are St. Paul's ever-present panhandlers. "They come to our store because there's so much action," Brenda said. "So they come, and we have to shoo them away all the time."

By visiting Candyland, people can carry on a tradition, she said. Customers are able to share with the next generation the same experience they had themselves. Instead of going to a convenience store and buying a candy bar produced in a factory far away, they visit Candyland and get homemade goodies and nostalgia candy. Great-grandparents take their great-grandchildren to the store, typically combining a trip to the Children's Museum or the Science Museum with a stop at Candyland. Some of them request candies that they remember from years ago, such as hard-to-find cream filberts—a creamed sugar wrapped around a filbert nut.

Longtime employee Laurie Johnson has waited on countless customers for whom a trip to Candyland offers a trip back in time. "My dad is ninety years old, and he remembers it from when he was a kid," Johnson said. "They have a good product. Their popcorn is awesome. There are not many places you can go to get fresh popcorn. It's an experience. The cliché about kids in a candy store is absolutely true. Even the adults can look at everything and have a hard time deciding. They say, 'What am I going to get? I need a minute.' In Arnie's day, we provided good services; prices were fair. With Doug and Brenda, they believe the customer comes first. You get awesome service there; their prices are fair."

Retiree Robert Kosmalski related how his brother, who met his wife at Bridgeman's on Seventh and St. Peter, now lives in Texas and makes a point of going to Candyland when he comes to

The store is bright with pink, red and white in February.

Minnesota for a visit. "He comes back carrying in one of their huge bags of caramel corn—and that's not the only attraction there. They have licorice snaps, the little tubular powdered licorice, and they have a lot of black licorice," Kosmalski said. "I have a friend much younger than I who says, 'Let's go grab a bag of caramel corn and watch a DVD.'"

Even though it's harder for them to get around, seniors who used to frequent St. Paul's theater district in the '40s and '50s still manage to get their hands on Candyland goodies. Retiree William Hunt of Grantsburg, Wisconsin, has a son who lives in the Twin Cities area, so he sent him on an errand one weekend. "I knew he was coming, and I said, 'Listen, go down to the popcorn store and get me a bag of the Chicago Mix popcorn and a bag of the caramel corn,'" Hunt said. He admitted somewhat sheepishly that the treats were gone within days. "I have many fond memories of that place over the years. My father, who had an office in St. Paul, frequently would come home with a bag of their goodies. It's a wonderful place."

Candyland's signature popcorn tins come in one- and two-gallon sizes.

Historian Gary Brueggeman admitted to being somewhat addicted to Candyland's chocolate-covered peanuts, and when his kids were young, he would look for excuses to bring them downtown so that he could visit Candyland.

"Considering where they are, I still can't believe it's still there. As you get older, that's the thing that's painful. The continuity of your past starts disappearing, but what makes you happy is when there are a few things that haven't changed," Brueggeman said. "There's a business or some place that's still there. There are so few of them, but to think that Candyland is still operating…it's like a little oasis, it's the last remnant of when downtown St. Paul was downtown, when it was alive, when people went there, when it was happening, when it was exciting."

He continued, "This is the thing that makes history so great. You have these little stories, but they reveal so much. They're so much bigger. History is a mosaic of all these people, and yet certain stories or businesses can capture a number of certain eras and persevere. It's an inspiring story, really."

Afterword

You park near the historic Landmark Center with its brownstone and turrets, where the streets converge at odd angles, leaving a small triangle for pedestrians to traverse. It's raining—a late March rain that aspires to become snow as the late afternoon darkens into dusk and the temperature slips. You tell your young teenager that you want to take her for a short walk, and you pull hoods over your heads. She tolerates this parental whimsy with nary an eye roll because she knows where you're going.

The lovely old Hamm Building offers a bit of shelter under storefront awnings. You take note of the throwback elegance of Heimie's Haberdashery—fedoras!—through the neat window display, and your child peeks into the swank interior of Meritage and expresses an interest in dining there sometime, much to your bemused surprise. As you pass through the arch that marks the entrance to the block-long Seventh Place and gaze at the folks enjoying themselves at Great Waters Brewing Company and Wild Tymes, you slow down and tell your kid about Old Seventh Street. These aren't your personal memories; you've been given the gift of others' stories, and you feel compelled to pass them on. It seems like the right thing to do.

Imagine that this street once went through—that there were no bookend office towers on either end of the block, you tell her.

Imagine streetcars and autos jamming this narrow street and people lined up to go to the movies there, on the right, at the Paramount and across the way on the left at the Palace/Orpheum. You point at the rows of windows running above the Palace Theatre and tell her that this building once was a hotel, the St. Francis, but that now those are apartments.

As you approach Wabasha, you say that the Walgreens on the corner has been there since the 1920s and that the store once had the coolest Art Deco neon sign ever. Too bad they didn't keep it.

Right about then, you smell it—a rich, almost burnt smell. Caramel. "I remember that smell!" says your teenager, who hasn't been down this way since she was Children's Museum age. All of a sudden, she's as excited as a preschooler. Mission accomplished.

You round the corner arm in arm and push open the door to Candyland.

Bibliography

Anderson, David, and Dave Moore. *Downtown: A History of Downtown Minneapolis and St. Paul in the Words of the People Who Lived It*. Minneapolis, MN: Nodin Press, 2000. This work is composed of excerpts from *The Alvin Karpis Story* by Alvin Karpis and Bill Trent (Coward McCann Geoghegan and Putnam Publishing Company, 1971), *VJ Day* by Elliott Tarbell (St. Paul Pioneer Press, 1945), *Bridgeman's* by Don Del Fiaco (St. Paul Pioneer Press, 1980) and *The Days of Rondo* by Evelyn Fairbanks (St. Paul: Minnesota Historical Society Press, 1980).

El-Hai, Jack. "One Smart Bookie." *The Atlantic*, May 2001.

Empson, Donald L. *The Street Where You Live*. Minneapolis: University of Minnesota Press, 2006.

Hess, Jeffrey A., and Paul Clifford Larson. *St. Paul's Architecture: A History*. Minneapolis: University of Minnesota Press, 2006.

Kenney, Dave. *Twin Cities Album: A Visual History*. St. Paul: Minnesota Historical Society Press, 2005.

———. *Twin Cities Picture Show*. St. Paul: Minnesota Historical Society Press, 2007.

Kunz, Virginia Brainard. *Saint Paul: The First 150 Years*. St. Paul, MN: Saint Paul Foundation, 1991.

Millett, Larry. *Lost Twin Cities*. St. Paul: Minnesota Historical Society Press, 1992.

Minnesota Public Radio. "Musicians Hope Local Jazz Is No Warm-up Act as Dakota Enters Artists' Quarter Space." April 7, 2014.

"Oliver Towne" (Gareth Hiebert). *Once Upon a Towne*. St. Paul, MN: North Central Publishing Company, 1959.

———. *St. Paul Is My Beat*. St. Paul, MN: North Central Publishing Company, 1958.

Pioneer Press. "Arnold Kelsey, Founder of Candyland Store." Obituary. April 4, 2004.

———. "Big-Hearted Downtown Grocers Moving On." November 12, 2013.

———. "Bittersweet Success." October 28, 1991.

———. "Candyland May Quit 7th Place, Contends Its Landlord Reneged." October 24, 1991.

———. "Chris Coleman: Investing in Arts and Culture: Next Up, The Palace Theatre, Downtown St. Paul." October 26, 2013.

———. "Downtown St. Paul Macy's to Close." January 2, 2013.

———. "For Palace Theatre Renovation, State Funding Sought." October 28, 2013.

———. "Grocer Fined for Wine Sale." August 4, 1967.

———. "Happy Birthday, Candyland." July 11, 2007.

———. "He Worked Downtown Selling Local Papers." January 16, 1996.

———. "Minnesota Children's Museum Optimistic Expansion Plan Will Get State Funding." April 11, 2013.

———. "Picture This: Downtown St. Paul's Lost Movie Theaters." November 1, 2009.

———. "Poker Players Lose with Police." March 14, 1958.

———. "Popcorn Shop to Stay, Expand Current Location." December 18, 1991.

———. "Three Bids Now in Play for 7th Place Buildings." June 30, 1999.

Star Tribune. "Apparently, Candyland Had Mega-Smells at Mall." January 31, 2003.

———. "Candyland Will Bring Its Sweet Treats to Stillwater." April 13, 2012.

————. "Customers Can Still Count on Candyland." March 25, 1996.

————. "Downtown St. Paul Should Do More to Love Me Back." December 15, 2002.

————. "Encore for 97-Year-Old Palace Theatre in Downtown St. Paul?" October 28, 2013.

————. "New Hope for Deserted Mall." February 19, 1990.

————. "Old and New Make Sweet Harmony at Candyland." December 15, 1997.

————. "Other Options for Historic St. Paul Block Getting a Look." May 21, 1999.

————. "Sale of 7th Place Residence One Step from Final Vote." July 27, 1999.

————. "A Shot in the Arm?" September 15, 1995.

————. "State Bonding Would Help Enlarge Crowded Children's Museum." April 12, 2013.

————. "St. Paul Beat: A Palace that's Fit for a Mayor." October 31, 2013.

————. "St. Paul Port Authority Committee Approves Purchase of Macy's Store." January 21, 2014.

Twin Cities Daily Planet. "Saint Paul's Tiny Candyland Stands Up to Corporate Snack Giants." January 23, 2012. tcdailyplanet.net.

Index

About the Author

S usan M. Barbieri is a St. Paul writer and longtime journalist who has worked for a variety of local and national publications, including the *St. Paul Pioneer Press*, *Minneapolis Star Tribune* and *Minnesota Monthly*.